The Ultimate Soul Journey

An Awakening to Spirit

An interdimensional journey with Angelic Guides, Ascended Masters, The Mary Connection, NDEs, Past Lives, Nature Spirits, Orbs, Light Spheres, Bigfoot, UFOs and The Source.

James Gilliland

First Printing, August 2007

Copyright 2016 by James Gilliland

Second Edition 2016

ISBN 978-1-329-84415-5

All Rights Reserved

Layout and Formatting: Aaron Rose

Printed in the United States of America

No part of this book may be reproduced in any form or by any electronic or mechanical means including information and retrieval systems without prior permission from the author in writing. For information concerning audiences with the author, workshops, and intensives or other printed or digital materials, contact:

ECETI

Phone: (509) 395-2092

Email: ecetireservations@gmail.com

YouTube: ECETI Stargate Official YouTube Channel

Website: www.eceti.org

Table of Contents

Appendix

Foreword

The Ultimate Soul Journey was not written for self-aggrandizement, but to share a path that many have taken, and bring understanding to some events in my life that were not only loving and blissful, but at times extremely challenging. There is a saying, "As one ascends into the planes of nirvana and bliss, not only are there tests, initiations and challenges, but the dark rises as well, to rear its ugly head in opposition."

In retrospect I would not change a thing, for the darkness has become a stimulus and teacher. When life rolls boulders it is best to build stairs, keeping one's eye on heaven. I would like to express heartfelt gratitude for everyone who made this dream possible. Be well.

James at Sattva Sanctuary
near Mt. Adams, Washington

1

Pre-Awakening

Birth and Reentry

My birth was not immaculate, but odd. My sister had been born just nine-and-a-half months earlier, which leads me to believe there was an intimate hospital visit to conceive me, or my parents were a bit amorous soon after leaving the hospital. My mother did not even know she was pregnant until I kicked her on the golf course; she thought her body was just adjusting after the last pregnancy.

I was a very large newborn at eight-pounds-plus, with a large head—much to the discomfort of my mother. I was so fat they called me "Buddha baby" and thought I would never walk.

At the age of two I remember being left alone in the front yard or atrium. I felt the cool lush dichondra and the rubber tree plant, and a strange feeling came over me, a feeling of "I am back. I made it, and now I have to survive until something unfolds." This profound feeling soon left and I fell into the childhood role I came to play.

It was a typical infancy and childhood until the age of five, when I came down with bronchial pneumonia. I was in the hospital, fading in and out of consciousness, scaring my parents half to death for fear of losing me. I was not afraid of death, because I was going back and forth between worlds anyway, and it seemed natural.

As I drifted, there was a woman in blue who kept coming to me. She was very loving and nurturing, and fed me ice cream. I did not know who this woman was; names were not important at that time, and all I remember is her loving presence and the ice cream. Later when asking who the lady in blue was, I was told there was not a woman dressed in blue attending to me and I could not have ice cream due to my condition. I did not know until later who she was (Mother Mary) and I dismissed it, as most children do when their parents or other adults tell them it was their imagination.

A Catholic Early Childhood

Due to my respiratory condition my parents, under the doctor's advice, moved to a small desert town in Apple Valley, California. I was extremely sensitive, and the air and consciousness of the city had seemed to make me ill. From that day on, in my new location, I never missed a day of school and was extremely healthy.

I went to a Catholic school because it was the only school in the high desert at that time. I did not have to attend the religious instruction and had a choice to attend or play outdoors, since my parents were not Catholic. I tried to sit through the indoctrination, but the outdoors kept calling me. It was a struggle with my guilt and fear that God might be upset or angry with me, but my friends outside won out. I spoke to my father about it, and the next day I could join my friends. I later found out it had to do with funding. They received government funding on the basis that they would not impose their beliefs on others.

I remember one day there was a friend of mine playing marbles. We sat down, drew the circle in the sand, and started firing at each other's marbles, trying to knock them out of the circle. Little did we know there would be others firing at us. There were a couple of boys who, after we were released from the religious indoctrination, decided we needed to be punished. They began throwing rocks at us, hitting my friend in the back and head. I quickly dispatched a rock of my own, which miraculously hit the one who had nailed my friend, right in the ear. He went down screaming and crying.

Next thing I knew, the priest had me by the ear, dragging me across the yard. I told him we were attacked first, that it was self-defense, but he kept yanking on my ear, and saying, "Come with me." I told him, "You are not God; Jesus would not do this," which only angered him more.

I sat in his office for a while and he went into the other room. Half an hour went by and then I was released. I went home and had a talk with my dad, due to a little note that had preceded me from the school office. I told him what had happened and he said, "It looks like there wasn't much more for you to do. Your friend was injured and you were being fired on." That was that.

My Earth Father

We lived at the base of a small mountain, with large granite boulders nearby. I spent most of my youth climbing and sitting on top of the monolithic boulders, wondering why people acted so strangely. Fortunately, there always seemed to be an inner voice which answered my questions. I wondered why people said one thing, felt another and then acted entirely incongruent with their thoughts, feelings and words. It made no sense.

The other thing I did not understand was the dishonesty and willful manipulation of others. My father, Jones Abner Gilliland, was a man of integrity. His word was law, and he kept it. He was very sensitive, not rigid, and to me he was a walking master. He was not religious; yet he lived a spiritual life. His passion was golf, and though he was a dentist by profession, he was also a no-handicap golfer. If not for his family obligations, I believe he would have been on the PGA circuit.

Some of his business partners would often take advantage of his trusting, giving nature and I could read them like a book. Some I refused, even as a child, to be around, because they merely acted like they cared about us, with phony affectionate displays, and gifts with ulterior motives.

We had a large piece of property in the desert, with over an acre of lawn. I remember some of my chores were to mow it and to weed and water the gardens and trees, along with various other odd jobs. I earned most of my childhood toys through allowances for doing chores, preparing me later for working in the adult world.

My parents had other properties that often needed carpentry, painting, and other repairs. This responsibility frequently fell on my shoulders. My father often referred to me as the rock of the family—always there and helpful whenever things needed to be done. My older brother was a master at disappearing.

Karma and My Big Brother

My older brother and I went through the typical sibling rivalries and power struggles. I had the gift of incredible hand-eye coordination. Everything I threw something at, I hit. We would often engage in sock fights, dirt-clod and sod wars. They would end in a couple of direct hits to his head or face, followed by a beating from him for my being the victor of the battle.

His karma always seemed to get the better of him. Once he was chasing me to prove his physical superiority, and he hit a stake in the ground, breaking his big toe. This created an abrupt end to the chase. Another time, at the age of seven, I was telling him that whenever he hurt others, his karma would punish him. He immediately slugged me and ran; then he looked back, only to smash his shoulder into the wall phone, knocking his feet out from under him and landing him flat on his back.

Ours was the typical brother relationship. He taught me a lot through example. He also had a strong yearning for Spirit. He went about the search in different ways, often experimenting with a drug or two. I would see him in his drug-induced "enlightened" condition, talking really slow, often in sentences that were nonsensical to me but to him were profound words of wisdom. I also saw a few of his friends who had come back from Vietnam having flashbacks and bad acid trips.

I am extremely grateful for witnessing this, because it pushed me into safe and natural ways of engaging other planes and dimensions. When a drug is in control, the participant is often out of control and can be blasted into planes of awareness without the proper tools or understandings. Being rocketed into a mental astral plane where thoughts manifest instantly, when one has a consciousness of fear and unworthiness or is unprepared or untrained, can be a hellish experience. Fortunately, my brother left drugs behind and went on to be a national champion in Tae Kwon Do, and today he is a very advanced healer, using various forms of breath work, process-oriented therapy and bodywork.

My "Great" Grandmothers

I remember spending time with my grandmother on my mother's side. To me, she was a saint. One day she asked me to take some old roses out to the garden. I did not know she wanted to compost them and so I planted them, not knowing any better. She walked out and I was all muddy and proud of the great job I had done. She laughed out loud, and rather than burst my bubble, she left the roses there and told me that I had done a really good job. Instead of pulling them up, she watered them along with all the other plants; they reminded her of my innocence and me at the time, as well as the joy and laughter it brought her to come out and see the roses neatly planted in a row.

Against all odds, the "dead" roses grew to become beautiful rose bushes. I think it was the love and joy she put into them, combined with the innocence of her grandson's youth, that made them grow.

She was always a positive influence in my life. While I was in the desert working as a carpenter I spent a lot of time with her.

My father's mother was also a very good influence. Although I did not spend much time with her, due to physical distances, she had quite an impact on me. She was a schoolteacher, sharp as a tack and self-assured. It was fun just listening to her stories and comments. She had a saying for everything. When crossing the desert she said it looked like hell's half acre—the devil's playground.

First UFO Sightings

One of the things I remember most about my brother is that we spent a lot of time sleeping outdoors, due to the desert heat. We had a large lawn, and at night we would lie there and stare up at the sky. There were often things overhead that we could not explain. They would zigzag, stop, and then zip off, disappearing into the heavens. We saw a mysterious blue light once, high in the sky, that we could not identify. It traveled very fast and kept ascending until it was out of sight.

A couple of times I felt something take me at night, and when I was brought back, my whole body was buzzing and paralyzed. I would try to move, yell or scream, but nothing could happen until the buzzing stopped. I would tell my mother and she would say it was just a dream.

One night there was a bright orange light high in the mountains. It lit up the entire valley, pulsing on and off as an orange glow, then it burst into a white light and disappeared. No one knew what it was. People went out to the area the next day, yet their search was to no avail.

My second major UFO sighting was in Mexico. I was with a few friends on a dock along the Rio Hardy River, just above San Felipe. We had been water-skiing most of the day. There was a rift going on between my best friend's girlfriend and myself. She was supposedly a very advanced water-skier and I had only water-skied one other time, which had been with my best friend Bill.

On that previous occasion, there were some very wealthy friends of my father who had invited us to go to Lake Havasu. Neither Bill nor I had any experience with water skis. The others were joking with their girlfriends and were going to make fools out of us. They gave us one ski, knowing we would fail and look foolish, and it would make them look all the better. One of the girlfriends went into the water with me and told me what to do. She also told me they were just trying to humiliate us.

Spirit seemed to have another idea, however. When the boat began to tow me, I popped right up, and once I felt comfortable, started swaying back and forth, jumping the wake. Soon I was making even harder and wider turns, lying really low. I overshot the beach a little and had to jump out of the ski and take a few quick steps to avoid a face full of sand, yet all in all, the rich boys' plan backfired.

Then it was Bill's turn. He followed suit, popping right up and making some really impressive turns. His landing, however, was a lot more professional than mine was. We thanked them for the ride, only to be accused of lying as to how many times we had been skiing. Both of us looked at them and said it wasn't that difficult; there was really nothing to it.

When we went to Mexico, Bill and his twin brother Bob had bought a ski boat and we were going to break it in. Right off the bat, Bill's girlfriend started challenging me to a contest. I did not see any point in it; it did not matter who was better, but if she needed to be better at something, that was all right by me. After hours of her insulting my abilities and making continuous challenges, I told her that if it would make her leave the matter alone and be quiet, I would accept her challenge.

We both took our turns skiing, with the people on the boat being the judges. To make a long story short, according to popular consensus and despite her beliefs that she had won, the vote showed clearly otherwise, in my favor. It also put Bill in a compromising position; to keep the peace with his girlfriend, he had to declare her the victor, despite what he knew to be true.

After dinner, we were celebrating a wonderful day of skiing on the river. Of course, I had to have a victory beer or two. We did not have a chance to become intoxicated, however, for we had just finished dinner when a strange sight appeared before all of us. It was a large orange luminescent ball of light, ascending on the other side of the river only a hundred yards away. It just hovered there for a while, then it rose at a 45-degree angle, suddenly jumping into what looked like hyper speed. It was a clear night and we followed the light for quite a while until it went out of sight into the heavens.

What was strange is that no one said a word until after it was gone. I asked the others, "Did you see that?" They said yes. I then asked, "What did you see?" I wanted them to verify what I had seen, not trusting my own two eyes. They described exactly what I had seen.

No one wanted to talk about it later. No one else would believe us, anyway. They would say it was just swamp gas. Things became really quiet, and the sighting was not mentioned again.

My Mother and Sisters, and a Past Life, Too

One of the things my brother would often do was instigate fights between my older sister and I, yet they did not last long, and we were usually very close. People often thought that she and I were fraternal twins. We spent a lot of time together, and we even lived together for a while after college. I enjoyed messing with her boyfriends' heads and was known to play a prank now and then.

When I was seven, my little sister was born. I remember her coming home all pink and wrinkly. I was assigned diaper duty occasionally, and she had the strange habit of farting just as I applied the baby powder. It was the highlight of the diaper duty.

Growing up as a child, I found that my mother was often distant and emotionally inaccessible. Though she was there for us physically, there was a gulf between us emotionally. I was often singled out and blamed for everything. The other siblings often received brand new gifts, while I ended up with the hand-me-downs.

My mother also had a habit of giving me something, but when I was at the height of my joy, it mysteriously disappeared. One gift was a drum set that vanished just as I was really getting into it. I watched my brother get a brand new bike, mini-bike, motorcycle, etc. He had a way of destroying things and passing down the wreckage to me. Both sisters were given brand new bikes, a horse, etc., and I would wonder what was wrong with this picture.

I would climb up to my granite boulder high above the desert floor and receive visions. I saw myself in Greece; my father had a family business, which was a combination store and restaurant. My current mother was my sister then, and when it came time to pass down the family business, it was given to me. My mother (as my sister) was very hurt and angry, for she had put as much work or more into the family business.

At the time it was customary to give the business to the son and a dowry to the daughter. I confronted my father in Greece about the unfairness of the custom, only to get a lecture about tradition. I realized my mother was acting out the pain of the past by withholding or taking things from me now that I loved; this allowed me to accept and depersonalize the situation.

This was my first lesson in past-life influences. They can create trauma and keep the circle of karma going if not forgiven, thus allowing the experience to settle into the soul as wisdom. I later confronted my mother for resolution. I had already forgiven the situation, but she was not ready to look at what had transpired and was unconscious as to her actions.

We often do things unconsciously, not even knowing why, or that the reasons for our present actions can be traced back to past-life influences. It took a while, but my mother began to open up a little at a time to the nature and importance of my work. She stepped in on two occasions to help financially with the Sanctuary and played a key role in its continuation. She also has a strong Mary connection, and I believe it was Mary who inspired her to act on these matters. She does not speak of it, yet deep inside she knows there is a greater plan unfolding.

Pranks, Etc.

I was very sensitive and guided as a child, plus I was very creative in the prank department. My brother and I were different, considering the mischief in which we often involved ourselves. He was spontaneous, and often got caught. I was more of a planner, and always had an escape route. The following story will illustrate this.

We had a very angry and controlling bus driver. On the last day of school we devised a plan. I was dropped off first, due to the age difference, and I found my strategic position, tomato in hand, waiting for the later bus which dropped off my brother. There was a house with dense vegetation just down the road, with an escape path leading up to the granite mountain.

The bus came rolling around the curb, with its diesel

engine thrumming and brakes squealing as it came to a stop. My brother got off, and the bus began its approach, shifting one gear after another, getting closer and closer to my hidden position. Just as it started to pass, I stood up and let the tomato fly. It was a cruise tomato, karmically guided to its appointed destination. The impossible shot found its mark, right through the little side window, splattering on the shoulder and neck of the driver. I was the hero that summer. Of course there was a little meeting the next year, in the principal's office, as to the origin of the tomato.

There were other small pranks, like putting fast-drying glue on the doorknobs of the classes we found boring. I had one very mean teacher in elementary school that shall remain nameless. One day I broke my leg playing baseball. I was leading off a base, waiting for the ball to come, and a friend was running full-speed for the base. He tripped and fell, landing on my leg and ankle. My foot swelled up immediately and I could not stand up; I tried and fell. Then that teacher picked me up, yelling at me, "You're not hurt. Stand up!" I fell again and she picked me up again, screaming "Stand up!"

Finally another teacher came up and intervened. He picked me up, put me on his shoulders, and carried me to the nurse's office. There they had to cut my shoe off. Later I was taken to the hospital and given a cast. There were pain pills as well, but for some reason, even as a child, I did not want them. I tried one and said, "No more."

Wompin

My parents' best friends lived in the city. We often visited there and stayed for weeks at a time. It was a mutual agreement that their kids would come up to the desert for a couple of weeks and we would go to the city.

The city created a whole new opportunity for mischief. We would often dress in black and sneak out at night to go out wompin. Wompin is when you throw oranges or lemons at cars till the police come. You chuck a few at them and then run through the backyards of several of your neighbors, jump in bed, and act as if nothing had happened.

We found our perch on top of a hill in a lemon grove, waiting for the first car. We would pick up old overripe lemons on the ground, stockpile them and lie in wait. It was a science. The first lemon would be thrown in a high lob. The second would be a little more direct and the third would be a line drive straight at the car. The trick was to have all three lemons land at the same time. Multiply that by five other participants, and you have a shower of lemons raining down on the unsuspecting victim. The other three boys of my parents' friends, at times accompanied by their little sister, made quite a team with me.

One particular night the police lay in waiting. When we began our wompin they seemed to come from all directions. There were headlights, spotlights and flashlights everywhere; our usual escape routes were cut off. We ran back and forth through the lemon grove, finally diving into some thorn bushes. The flashlights and spotlights were going back and forth, and the police were shouting, "Give it up. We know where you are."

The officers, who were on our usual escape path, walked right up to our bush, saying, "We know you are in there. We are going to start shooting if you don't come out." We sat there shaking, scared out of our wits. I heard some rustling in the bush next to me, and there right at my feet was a very large skunk. The skunk miraculously headed out of the bushes, right towards the police. I sat motionless, praying that the skunk would not take an offensive posture at us. As it turned out, the police were bluffing, and the skunk gave them the inspiration to move on.

When the police passed us, we bolted down the trail as fast as we could run. There was a younger cop who took off after us. He made it over the first fence, hot on our trail. We knew the route, however, which was to our advantage. He made it over the second fence, hot in pursuit. He did not know what was behind the third fence. The third backyard not only had a German shepherd, which knew us, for we often played with it and fed it, but the yard also had a lot of staked and wired-down fruit trees. The cop hit the first wire, spinning him around, and the second wired tree grabbed his ankles, laying him flat out, looking up to be greeted by a large German shepherd which was not happy about his presence. There was a lot of growling and scrambling on the other side of the fence as we snuck in the back door, tore our clothes off, and jumped into bed.

Shortly afterward, the door opened, and there were two large officers with my friends' mother standing in front of them. She turned on the light and said, "See, officers, they are asleep." My friend gave an award-winning performance, rolling over in a half-asleep voice, groaning "Turn out the light." The police officers promptly left, and that was the end of my wompin career.

Bob the Dummy and His Daughter

The next creative adventure involved dummies. We found a tree with a large limb overhanging across the road and created a dummy, stuffing Levi's and a shirt with rags, cotton, etc. We called him Bob. He had socks for feet and a stuffed Halloween mask for a head.

We had a lot of fun with Bob. Bob used to love to swing from a tree and land flat out on the hood of an oncoming car. He also used to love to get beaten up and tossed off a cliff or three-story building in the presence of onlookers. Of course, Bob had a mind of his own and we had nothing to do with his mischievous behavior. He put us up to it.

The creation of Bob led to Bob's daughter. Bob's daughter was a doll that you strapped to your feet and danced with. It was my friend's little sister's doll, and she gladly offered it to us if she could hang out with us. We found an old tricycle and used the straps on the doll's feet to secure it to the pedals. We then wired the handlebars to the back so that the tricycle would go straight. It was hilarious to see the tricycle going down the road, the doll's legs pedaling as fast as they could, being secured to the pedals. The doll had a little bonnet and a dress, and the movement made it so lifelike, it could be easily mistaken for a little girl on a tricycle. It was great for staging mock accidents.

We found the perfect road with a sufficient slope, tied a fishing line to the back of the tricycle, and let it go out into the street. Drivers would hit their brakes, jump out, and begin lecturing the doll. One woman hit the tricycle, bent it up a bit, and said "Oh my God!" over and over, only to see the doll's raggedy face smiling up at her. She offered a few choice words in our direction and left.

The last we saw of Bob's daughter was late one evening, when a drunk driver was swerving down the lane. We played out the fishing line, and Bob's daughter started her descent down the road. The drunk did not even stop until he hit the tricycle. He slammed on his brakes, but it was too late for Bob's daughter, as the tricycle was crushed under the grille of the oncoming car. To our surprise, rather than stopping and getting out, the drunk hit the gas and sped off, dragging the tricycle and doll off into the sunset, grinding sparks all the way. I think that was his twelve-step program all condensed into one step.

My Critter Friends in the Desert

The rest of my childhood was spent mostly in the desert, catching lizards and snakes. We had several cages where we kept various pets. We often surprised our mother with a large chuckwalla (which is a lizard the size of a Gila monster) or a snake or two.

One day we brought home a huge scorpion. It was the granddaddy of all scorpions. When we rolled over its log den, rather than scurry off, it challenged us, raising its large claws in defiance. We ran home, got a big Tupperware bowl, tossed it over the scorpion, and slid the lid under it. We were proud of our catch, and found a large cardboard box to keep it in.

My mother, upon seeing our new pet, went berserk. She got a full can of Raid and let the scorpion have the whole thing, which didn't even faze it. She hit it with a broom handle and the critter was so tough it bounced off. Next came the shovel. We watched in sadness, and could not come to the aid of the poor scorpion. I guess when mothers get into protection mode, you just have to get out of the way. We decided after that to let the rattlesnakes go.

The chuckwallas, very large non-poisonous lizards, made great pets. You could tame them down and hand feed them. We used to rub their bellies and put them to sleep. We had one chuckwalla astronaut that used to ride one of our kites. He would go up out of sight, strapped in his little harness, and return cold, but okay. I always wondered if he went back to the other chuckwallas and told them his story of what happened. I can hear it now: "I was just sunning myself on a rock when this huge being appeared out of nowhere, grabbed me, rubbed my belly and put me in a trance, put me in confinement, then flew me high above the valley and let me go."

My father taught us to hunt and fish, as well as to know which snakes and insects were poisonous. We went barefoot and in cutoff jeans most of the time. He said we were so much like Indians that he took us down to the barbershop and gave us Mohawk haircuts. My mother made it very clear this was not appropriate, for she was very much into outer appearances and what the neighbors would think. Actually, we had no neighbors, except for one little old lady across the way.

We also had a horse named Mrs. Ed. She was very gentle and understanding. We fell off her all the time and she would stop and wait for us to get back on, and she made sure she didn't step on us. We didn't have a saddle, but rode bareback or with a pad.

One day while pregnant with Jeopardy, she got angry with my father and bit him. He was pushing her around while we were cleaning the stall. At the time he weighed around 240 pounds, and she picked him up right off the ground. It was the first time I saw my father react violently in anger. He almost knocked the horse out with a punch to the head. He later had huge black and blue welts on his side where he was bitten.

Our horse gave birth to a colt that we named Jeopardy, because he was so ornery you were in jeopardy just entering the corral. One day he backed me into a fence, kicking me over and over, bruising my arms as I blocked the kicks. It was a real lesson in awareness concerning how to sense the intent of an animal.

We lived close to a golf course, and I spent a lot of time golfing with my father. At the age of nine I was entered into a tournament called the Wildflower Tournament. I won my division and the next two age divisions up. I placed second in the eighteen-year-old division and they pulled my father aside and said, "You know, we have to give him all the trophies, according to the rules." My father said that this would deprive the other children and he would have a talk with me. It was unimportant to me, because even as a child, all I cared about was that other people were happy. I took only the trophy for my age division.

I had two fights in junior high school, both of which I am not proud. I did all I could to avoid them, yet in both cases the boys were bullies, and the more I avoided them, the more I was hassled. The first ended up being more of a wrestling match, with a couple of punches. I won by pinning and restraining my opponent until he gave up. After the fight was finished, rather than feel victorious, I felt sorry for him.

The second was a little more severe, and I ended up punching him in the stomach, dropping him to his knees, crying. There was no victory in that either, and again I felt both anger at having been put in that position and sorrow for causing someone pain. I vowed never again to strike another person. What was funny was that I never had to fight after that, for word got around school concerning the event.

High School Highs and Lows

In high school I was not unlike most other kids. I was captain of the water polo team, but the competition killed the fun and I quit the team to work at a local market. Quite frankly, I found high school very boring and uninteresting, due to all the recycled ignorance and programming being taught. Basically, I attended in order to meet and be with my friends. I cruised through, doing only what was necessary, leaning towards biology.

Even when I was a small child, my report card was sent home, saying, "We are worried about James. He seems to spend more time with snakes, lizards and other animals than with people." My biology teacher stood up one day and said, "I will give extra-credit points for anyone who brings in an unusual pet to share with the class." Little did he know, at the time I had a horned owl I was rehabilitating, plus a very large Southern Pacific rattler, not to mention a few other pets.

I showed up with the owl and a very large snake. His eyes got as big as saucers and he said, "I think there are rules against having these on the school grounds." He made a quick phone call to the front office for permission and returned. The rattlesnake cage had a lock on it, so it was all right. The owl had a stand and jesses to tie it down.

The biology teacher, not wanting to miss the opportunity to share with the rest of the students, accepted the two pets into the main lab. I told him that if he was to take the owl off the stand, I needed to be there; it did not trust anyone else. He did not believe me, and during his next class he went out to the lab, grabbed the glove I had left, and untied the owl. The owl made an immediate escape, tipping over Petri dishes and beakers, eventually knocking out one of the ceiling panels and escaping into the roof of the school.

I was called out of my next class to come get my owl out of the roof. There was a ladder there, and I put on the glove, lifted my hand up through the ceiling, and the owl gently landed on it. After tying the owl back to its perch, I turned to the teacher, who was a bit flushed, and I repeated, "He does not trust just anyone. Please do not untie him unless I am here." I smiled and went back to my room, chuckling as soon as I rounded the corner.

In high school I was awkward with women. I was very short until my sophomore year, when I grew seven and a half inches. There was one particular young woman of whom I was very fond. She ignored me until I grew, then she decided she had to have me. By then I had given up, due to all the earlier rejection, and I realized that if height was all that had stood between us before, it was too shallow of a relationship for me.

There was another young woman I had a deep crush on, but no matter how hard I tried to make it work or connect, it wasn't meant to be. I spent most of my time at the beach, bodysurfing in the summers, hoping to unite with one of those bronze beauties on the beach.

I was in a car accident during my junior year, which really wasn't an accident. I was out drinking on Halloween night; I was not drunk but had had a couple of beers, and we were driving to another party when our car was hit with eggs. We went back later with water balloons, and the people that had egged us were standing in the street. What I did not know was that an undercover officer was questioning them.

As I passed by, I flung a water balloon over the car roof, while driving to the other side of the street. It found its mark directly on the back of the head of the officer. A high-speed chase began through three counties, ending up with my car "mysteriously" hitting two poles and a brick wall, all of which seemed to just jump right out in the road. That was how I saw it anyway, after a few beers and being in complete denial. The car was completely totaled, and I spent the night in jail.

When put in the cell, I saw there was a man there who was strung-out on drugs. He asked, "What are you in here for?" I said, "I hit a narc in the head with a water balloon." My new roommate broke out in a loud belly laugh, reared his head back, and kept laughing until he fell flat out on the floor.

I called the guard and told him what happened. He asked me if the guy was still breathing. I looked down and could see his chest moving. The guard said, "He will be all right, with a reminder in the morning concerning what he did the night before."

That was my criminal experience in the Big House. It took me quite a while to shake off the guilt from acting so stupidly and wrecking the car. My father showed me how disappointed he was, but he could tell I had already been through a lot. He knew that leaving me there in jail all night, with the worry and the torment, as well as the feeling of disappointing him and losing my car, was enough. I was grounded for quite a while in order to think about the experience. It really sobered me into becoming a lot more responsible.

A Dog Called Dammit

One day my father brought a dog home, a cross between a black Lab and a Springer spaniel. It was a large dog, with the hair and markings of a Springer spaniel and the body of a Lab. I loved that dog as a friend, raised it like a little brother, and we were often seen wrestling on the lawn together. I would growl at him, attack, and he would growl back. It looked as though I was being mauled, but it was all in fun. To top it off, when he got out of the yard, my little sister would go up and down the neighborhood yelling "Daammit, here Daaaammmmit!"

My mother was upset about the uncivilized way we behaved with the dog. After all, what would the neighbors think, with her son acting like a common animal and her daughter screaming "Dammit!" at the top of her lungs?

I went to Mexico on a trip and found upon my return that Dammit was gone. My mother had given my dog away to a rancher, and refused to tell me where he lived. It was like losing a brother; I felt betrayed on the deepest level.

Later my mother tried to replace Dammit with a golden retriever named Reja. Reja was with me for 21 years. We were so close that we could perform psychic dog tricks. I carried her in my jacket when she was a pup, until one day she decided to relieve herself. I guess it was time she walked on her own.

One day seveal years ago, in rural Washington State, I looked out my window and saw Reja sitting with three coyotes. I went and joined her. We all meditated together, and it was just like the telepathic connection I had with her. The coyotes and I cut a deal: They could run the ranch for gophers and mice, but had to leave the chickens alone. They honored it. While the chickens free-ranged, having the run of the ranch, the coyotes also walked the grounds. It was not uncommon to see them peering in the window, with their paws on the sill.

Developers later moved in and raped their hunting grounds, shooting everything that moved. I have found animals to be much more honorable than humans. It is a shame that we humans cannot keep our word as a family, like coyotes do. I often wonder who is the more evolved? Living in harmony in a complementary relationship with nature is something that few humans can comprehend.

Perpetual College

After high school I went on to college. I was on the ten-year program, changing my major from year to year. I started in pre-law, took pre-dental, and then ended up taking all the courses to become an X-ray technician. I took philosophy, and the teacher taught us that when you are dead you are dead—game over.

I took psychology and it was really limited, because everything went back to childhood and some Freudian complex, ignoring what I knew even as a child—that much of our problems come from past lives as well. I argued with the teachers about the out-of-body experiences I'd had as a child, saying, "I know we are a spirit, and that spirit is eternal." There is much more to us than our childhood.

In chemistry I kept asking, "What is beyond the atoms, elements and molecules? Who created them?" The chemistry professor became very irritated, and flunked me. Even physics was boring. I would argue the fact that what we are really looking at is a lot of empty space concerning matter, which was here only half the time. It was alternating back and forth from a particle to a wave. I kept saying that everything we think is real seems to have no basis in reality; it is only energy, which is lowered from light...but what is beyond the light? What set it all into motion? What is the intelligence behind all of this? Of course this is a non-scientific question, and it's improper to ask teachers questions they cannot answer. Nonetheless, I was not a very good student when it came to absorbing the recycled ignorance without question.

In college I dated a woman named Amy. She seemed to lack honesty, and needed more than one man in her life, in order to fill her emptiness. It was a roller-coaster relationship of lies and deceit. I would forgive her and she would lie and deceive, until I had finally had enough. To her, men were trophies to lie with and brag about later.

It was a lesson in discernment, because I had no idea that people were capable of such dishonesty and betrayal. I had projected qualities onto her which she did not possess. It is hard, sometimes, to accept the fact that your lover just might not be all you wish them to be.

Later in my life a Master said to me, "Trust is earned." I now know what he meant.

Chasing the Dollar

I decided then that the only reason for my college education was to make money. Real estate would give me enough money to have the free time to do what I really wanted to do, which was to be outdoors and travel. I studied and passed the real estate courses with flying colors, and got my license. I also went to broker's and contractor's school. I was very handy with my hands and remodeled plenty of houses, doing various odd jobs. This seemed to complement the real estate work.

Then I met a beautiful woman named Sharon, who worked for my father. We hit it off immediately and began dating. We lived together for quite some time and shared many wonderful moments.

If asked if there was one thing I could do all over again, it would have been to end things differently with her. There were many personal problems that I will not go into; I decided to end our relationship, out of respect for her. We parted, not because I did not love her, but because I was not ready to make a commitment.

Becoming tied to a nine-to-five job, the white picket fence or condo, just did not work for me. There was a deep yearning within my soul to do something different. I could not be trapped into the false security of social consciousness. A larger calling was tearing at me inside, but I did not know what it was. All I knew was that I was not ready, and to this day there are times when I think back to the love we shared, how well we got along, and how giving she was. Sharon, if you are out there, from the bottom of my heart I am sorry for any pain I might have caused you...

Later I went into selling houses, and was trained with a company that shall remain anonymous. They put me through their course that showed you how to manipulate people into buying what they really didn't want in the first place. It was all about agreeing with them, diverting their attention, and redirecting their desires. I said, "Wouldn't it be more appropriate to just find them what they wanted, filling their needs?" Of course my comment went over like a lead balloon and I was branded a troublemaker, because they did not like the mirror, which reflected back to them their own lack of integrity.

I soon left that office and went to work for the same commercial real estate firm where my mother worked, since they needed help. There I was rubbing shoulders with the big boys. They were multimillionaires, owning large shopping centers, office buildings and chain stores. What I realized there was that you had to stay on your toes. Everyone had a lawyer, everyone was trying to screw the other guy and keep from being screwed. It was dog-eat-dog with little honesty or integrity, and your word meant nothing unless signed and notarized.

The owners retired and we ended up with the business, and later my mother retired as well. I was now living high on the hog, had two cars, a four-bedroom house, prestige and position.

I was even on the board of the Chamber of Commerce. There I received a first-hand experience concerning the nature of city politics. I was shocked at the decision-making process, how corrupt it was, and how uneducated and unethical the people were on the board. It had very little to do with service, and everything to do with hidden agendas.

I was contemplating, "Is this all worth it?" Although I was a success, I was not happy, and the love and joy in my life was almost nonexistent. Soon afterward is when the near-death experience happened.

2

Awakening

Nature's Hand in Awakening

I was out bodysurfing with a friend named Chris. We were far out on a sandbar, body-surfing in six-foot to occasional nine-foot waves. At the time I thought I was invulnerable, having been on the water polo and swim teams in high school and spending a lot of my life in the water, since I was an avid swimmer. I could also do three laps underwater in an Olympic-size pool. It was like going into a state of suspended animation while still swimming.

What we had not planned for on that day were the sneaker waves that came in without warning. The waters started rushing out, and far off, rolling toward land, was a great wall of water forming. As we saw it coming, I was further inland, due to having just ridden a wave. We both started swimming as fast as we could to get through or over it before it broke. The water rushed out so fast that rather than swimming, I was partially hitting the sand as I stroked frantically to get over or beneath the approaching wave. I didn't know whether to try to run in waist-deep water, or swim.

Chris was further out, and he barely made it over the wave before it crested. I was not so lucky; it broke right on top of me. I found out what it feels like to be a fly after the swatter has found its mark. The wave hit me so hard that it dislocated my shoulder and crushed my diaphragm.

It tumbled me over and over, holding me under for what seemed like an eternity.

When I finally surfaced, I could not swim very well or breathe. I kept trying again and again to breathe, but had had the wind knocked out of me. Just as I was about to get my first breath, the next wave found its mark, crashing down on me, pulling me under again and holding me for what seemed like forever.

When the third wave came crashing down, I knew my life was over. There was nothing else I could do, and I surrendered. I remember taking one breath underwater, letting go of the pain of holding my breath. Suddenly a warm feeling came over me. I surrendered to the feeling and began to move upward.

Greeting the Source: My Near Death Experience

There was a tunnel of light as I moved upward. I very quickly passed what seemed to be many planes and dimensions; I did not stop to talk. I ended up in a golden plane of pure consciousness and energy. The love, joy, security and bliss were beyond words. It was as if I was held in the arms of God.

I was still conscious of myself in the light, and there was a greater consciousness surrounding me. A conversation took place, thought-to-thought transmissions going on inside of me. I asked the presence, "How can I stay?"

The thought came back to me, "I have never told one of my children when to come or go; that is free will."

I asked again, "How can I earn the right to stay?" I was obviously still dealing with concepts and programming from some of my Catholic upbringing.

The thought came to me again, saying, "You cannot earn what is given freely and unconditionally."

I floated in the light for some time after that. Feeling overwhelmed with the loving presence I asked, "How can I serve?" There was no answer.

I waited for quite some time, remaining in complete bliss, when finally the thought came into my mind, "What brings you joy?" I was thinking that God had some major plan all worked out for me, and I was shocked to realize that all God wanted was for me to be happy. I had to make the choice myself to serve.

I said, "What would bring me joy is to return and teach others the true nature of God. There are so many images, wrathful misperceptions, fear, guilt and unworthiness."

The last words I heard were: "As you wish."

Back on the Planet

The next thing I remember was feeling my leg hit the sand and a man grabbing me by the shoulder, pulling me up onto the beach. He said, "Are you all right?" I said yes, although I was slipping in and out of consciousness. He left me to go help others.

There had been some people out on the jetty fishing when the waves moved in, sweeping them into the ocean. Many were caught off-guard that day and the rescues were still going on. I crawled up on the beach and passed out, only to wake up later with a lifeguard calling my name from a Jeep's loudspeaker. I looked down and there was a puddle of water that had come from my lungs; I was still sick and disoriented. I waved at the lifeguard and told him I was James, but I could not stand up.

He walked up to me and asked, "Do you know where your buddy is?" I said no. I then received a stern lecture about the buddy system.

When he finished, I looked up at him and said, "Right now I barely even know who I am."

The lifeguard finally realized I did not look too well. I

told him that I myself had almost drowned, was pulled in, and passed out.

The last thing I had remembered was seeing Chris go over the first big wave. He had made it. I did not know till later that he was clinging to a buoy, was knocked off it, and then was thrown over the jetty, receiving massive abrasions, bruises and cuts. A helicopter picked him up and flew him to the hospital, where he was being stabilized.

The lifeguard gave me directions to the hospital and asked me if I was all right to drive. I said yes, but wasn't. I grabbed Chris's keys and our things and made my way to the car. It was then that I noticed I was very unsteady on my feet. I had a sickening feeling in my stomach, followed by a flushed sensation. I could function, but not very well. I made it to his car, started it up and headed for the hospital, which was not too far away, and the route was well marked.

I went to the emergency room, where I was met by a nurse who said, "Come with me quickly." She told me she needed someone to keep talking to Chris, someone familiar so that he would not go into shock.

They were dressing his wounds, and my compassion and empathy upon seeing him were overwhelming. I continued to talk to him, but I could not see. My vision just went black. I held onto a chair, though I did not feel like I was going to pass out; I just could not see. I think my senses were on overload and the eyesight just shut off.

I stayed until he was stabilized and his mother came; then I made my way to the waiting room. A nurse asked me if I was all right and helped me to find a chair and sit down. I stayed there for a while until my vision returned.

A little while later, his mom came into the waiting room, very upset. I told her what happened and that there was nothing anyone could have done. As far as Chris and I were concerned, the score was nature 2, us zip, and we were both extremely humbled.

I visited him later and it was hard for me to see him all bandaged up. He looked like the Mummy. I told him he ought to write a book, "How to get Moore out of body-surfing," being as that was his last name. He laughed and cringed at the same time, due to the stitches.

Reevaluation Time

While Chris was recuperating, I was reevaluating my life. I was dating a woman at the time and she was running me around in circles. She would make dates, break them, and tell me she wanted to see some other guy in a band. I was head-over-heels in love but it was not reciprocated.

We went out to dinner and she started up with the same old drama, breaking some plans we had made earlier and saying she wanted to date others. Somehow there was no more emotional charge concerning the game being played. I was not jealous, angry or hurt, and a strange warm glow descended upon me. I looked her straight in the eye and said, "As you wish." It was as if I had ascended back into the golden light. There was no attachment, just love.

With me not playing the game, she got very confused, even angry. She said, "You have changed; you're different."

I told her, "Yes, I have changed; if you want to be with me in a loving relationship, with honesty and integrity, working towards building a future, great. If you want to continue with breaking dates and dishonoring the relationship, it is time for us to part."

She tried again to make me angry and jealous by telling me she wanted to date the guy in the band. I told her, "If that is what you want, you should do it."

That was our last dinner. The real estate job also soon came to a close. I was different. I could feel and sense everything. The motives and intentions of the people around me, as well as the vibrations of their attitudes and emotions, were making me ill.

I was now awake in the sea of confusion and lack of

love, joy and integrity in the world in which I lived. It was then that I realized that material objects possess no love, joy or emotions. These emotions are all felt within.

My Inward Education from Jesus

In my dreams and meditations, Jesus would often come to me. I would receive valuable insights as to many of my worldly challenges. I was also escorted to other worlds for a greater understanding of the multidimensional multiverses in which we live.

I was told there is a vibrational continuum, and that all thought, attitudes and emotions have a frequency or vibration. The attitudes, emotions and beliefs in the world in which we live establish our vibration, and we are known throughout the universe by our vibration; it is our personal signature.

I was also shown how people of like vibration, with similar fears, wounds and traumas, as well as beliefs and desires, gravitate to each other. They act as mirrors, to help each other evolve.

The highest vibration is pure unconditional love, joy and bliss. The highest heavens are occupied by beings that emanate this consciousness in the highest expression. The lower vibrational attitudes and emotions are fear, anger, jealousy, greed, selfishness and separation. There are many levels in-between.

There are not just heaven or hell; there are levels of consciousness—planes and dimensions and even planets within them where whole civilizations of people exist. I was shown a lower level where malevolent spirits reside. They were grossly disfigured, their auras were dark, murky-colored and often gray, and their outer expression matched their consciousness. The fear, anger, lashing out and trying to control and dominate each other was not a pretty sight. I was told they were not condemned to that plane; they were magnetized there according to their consciousness. That is where they have chosen to express. At any time, once they have had their fill of this expression, they can receive healing and help, moving up to higher levels, but it must be according to their will and desire.

I saw light beings waiting to minister to them once they chose a higher path of expression, yet they were not aware of the beings' presence until the choice was made. I was taken to less-malevolent planes, where the struggles for power were continuing and people were still trying to manipulate and control each other, but in more subtle ways. This level also had gray, murky energies, yet not as dark as the first level. There were all kinds of dramas being acted out, with psychic bonds and cords attached to each other, as each tried to gain love, joy, security and happiness from the other people.

As I moved up the vibrational continuum, there was less fear, anger and the need to control or manipulate. People were more loving, caring and service-oriented. The colors had lost their murkiness and there was a greater light.

The more one evolves spiritually, the more one moves into service, for the flow of love, joy and bliss that moves through one while serving others is the grandest treasure of all. Further up the continuum, there were people who had almost mastered judgment. However, they still had some religious or cultural orientation and belief that separated them from the whole. There were people devoted to their masters, names, images and doctrines. They were good people, yet would not accept any other path to God; thus they isolated themselves on lesser planes. There were wonderful guides and teachers on these planes, yet they were still stuck on the wheel of death and rebirth because they had not yet mastered the consciousness necessary to ascend.

Beyond the wheel of life and death, beyond the astral levels, was the Christ Consciousness. There I met great avatars, masters, saints and sages from every culture and belief who had mastered judgment and transcended all religious and cultural barriers, into a universal love for all people and all life. They were exquisitely beautiful, the colors were brilliant, and they saw the Creator within all Creation, including themselves. They were one with the one consciousness that encompasses all consciousness on all planes and dimensions throughout the universe. There were beings of an even greater expanded awareness of love, joy and bliss that were universal and cosmic in nature. Their very being took up whole planets, universes and multiverses.

I was told that the keys to ascension are so simple that very few can master them. They get caught up in intellectual, complicated systems and structured truths, which they often defend, creating even more separation and division.

The path is simple: Focus on pure unconditional love, joy and bliss until you become it. Keep your eye fixed on this goal and be kind to yourself, others and all life. This allows one to expand along the vibrational continuum into higher, more expanded states of awareness.

I was also told the key to mastering judgment is seeing the Creator in all Creation and purposeful good in everything. This does not mean dropping discernment. You can discern the nature of a person or an event without judgment, and choose not to participate.

The last thing I was told is that being a Christ does not mean being a doormat. Send a blessing to those with whom you do not resonate, and move on. My greatest teachings were the ones that taught me to allow.

Off to the Desert

I left the real estate office, sold everything, and went to the high desert to be a carpenter. My first job was building prefabricated homes. We built them first at a factory and then moved them up to the desert.

While assembling the homes in the desert, I found myself being both an on-site carpenter and a security guard. There were times when we had to wait for materials or for part of the house to come, and I was the only one on the site. I would take the lunch I had packed and share it with the chipmunks and birds.

After a while, I noticed the birds and the chipmunks had distinct personalities; I could even sense their mindsets and feelings. For a while, this made me question my own sanity. I knew how each animal would react, which one was the bully, which one was young and inexperienced, how the females were distinct, etc. I realized animals had souls as well, though of a different order, and if we did not judge them we could communicate through feelings.

My parents had an office building they wanted remodeled, and my previous skills as a carpenter and contractor in commercial real estate qualified me for the job. The job included a large addition of several other offices.

My folks received several bids; I offered the lowest and began to line up subcontractors. When completed, the office building was well under the lowest bid, to the tune of $60,000. I had also added many extras—landscaping, automatic lights and sprinklers, and rear parking, all of which were not on the original plans. We also did a lot of tenant improvements.

Upon completion I was told that, rather than receive the $60,000 surplus, I would get the $4,000 truck we had purchased to do the job, plus the small amount of money I had received to cover expenses while building.

I had gone deep into debt, thinking I would receive a large bonus at the end. Rather than getting so much as a pat on the back, I was criticized for not finishing faster. I would have been happy with just a token sum to clear my debts, with a little extra to get started on another adventure, giving the rest back to my family.

There were a few comments on how long the job had taken, even though it was finished on schedule. There had been only one delay, due to my mother's brother, a plumber, who had made a mistake in placing a roof drain. He refused to fix it, the inspector refused to sign off on it, and I was caught in the middle. There was a power struggle over moving the roof drain.

I felt completely crushed by the lack of appreciation from my parents. I knew it was my mother who controlled the purse strings, and her wounds from the Greek life were playing out again. Again I do not hold any grudges, and my mother came through later in assisting the Sanctuary. Everything balances out in the end. There is a saying, "You can never take anything from another or keep what is not yours. All will balance in the end."

I packed my bags and headed north.

Santa Cruz Shake-up

I moved to Santa Cruz in Northern California to be with my brother. He had an import shop, and I spent time back and forth between the mountains and the beach. The majestic redwoods were wonderful and provided a loving shelter for me to rethink and heal my wounds. I worked in the shop at just above minimum wage, as well as picking up a few carpentry jobs here and there.

The import shop was in the hole and wasn't doing very well. I watched the inventory as it sold and told the owners that carvings and exotic hard goods were not selling—that it was the dresses from Bali that were the big sellers. If we reduced the space for the carvings and made more room for dresses, we would do better.

I remodeled the store, built new racks, and we brought in more dresses from Bali and India. Sales started to skyrocket. Soon we were too small, and needed a larger location. Chuck, my brother's partner, soon became a close friend of mine and was very appreciative of the insights and work I was doing.

I was made manager, given a small raise and we moved to a much larger location. There we completely remodeled the store, building more racks and focusing primarily on clothing, with the carvings in the window to dress up the clothing displays. We also imported sweaters from Mexico for winter, and between the sweaters, jackets from Bali and carvings, we did well in the winter, especially around Christmas.

Business was booming, and Chuck decided he wanted to make me a partner. I continued to help the store grow, putting my heart and soul into it. However, there was a rift between my brother and Chuck. My brother was never there, off vacationing or on a buying trip, leaving all the work to the partner and me. It was not unlike my childhood. This was upsetting Chuck, and rather than face my brother, he turned his anger and disappointment on me. When my brother returned, I found out I was no longer a partner. If I wanted to be a partner, I would have to take it out of my brother's half.

The store had gone from the red to grossing well over $300,000, and sales were still climbing. That was when greed set in, and soon it was made clear that my presence there was no longer needed. I had worked very hard for years, putting in long hours to build the business.

This was the second major betrayal in my life. My mother had betrayed my trust by not paying me for remodeling the office building; now my best friend and my brother were fighting at my expense. No matter what I tried to do to heal the situation and show that their argument was between them and should not be to my detriment, the colder the shoulder I received. My entire support system, both emotional and financial, was undermined, and soon afterward I experienced a major back injury, laying me flat out for a month and a half. Later I learned that the decision to ace me out of the store was due to greed on Chuck's part.

The Hardest Lesson: Forgiveness

I refused to be a victim. I knew about karma and the fact that consciousness creates reality. Having my emotional and financial support ripped out from under me again, it manifested in my lower back. I suffered severe damage to a disk and was even told by a chiropractor, most of who are usually against operations, that my only options were an operation or a wheelchair.

I lay in bed for a month and a half, praying, begging and demanding a healing. I tried everything; I knew I was not going to have an operation and I would heal it myself, even if it took years.

There were times when I had no food, because I could not get up on my own. The mere act of turning over in bed caused incredible pain. I had lost the feeling and use of my right leg, and things were not looking good. Rather than go into fear or become a victim, I prayed. Soon after that, someone would show up and ask, "Can I get you something to eat?"

Little by little I began to move around. I would roll over and crawl to the bathroom, which was a monumental feat in itself. I would also open the refrigerator and grab whatever was in there that I could reach to eat.

After a while I could get up with the use of crutches and make my way to the bathroom or get a quick meal, but I was very limited as to the amount of time I could stay up. Soon the crutches were traded for a large staff, which acted as my right leg, the limb that was just beginning to show some signs of life.

Day by day, I could stand for longer and longer periods of time. I went in for several chiropractic adjustments, but then could no longer afford them. I lay there, contemplating my creation, and felt there was a victim pattern that was being acted out, some self-worth issues, etc.

I was told by my brother that it was my karma, yet I felt there was more. He was not taking responsibility for his participation, which seemed to be a recurring event.

Others were saying "You created it somewhere; you did this to them, and it is coming around." This, as well, seemed off the mark. I was fully aware that consciousness creates reality, yet I could not access any memories of where I had done harm in the past to the people involved, during this life or others.

I had plenty of time to contemplate the situation, for I was going nowhere. Finally in a deep meditation it occurred to me: forgiveness. I had not fully forgiven the other betrayals and was still carrying a charge, which was recreating the event. It was not something I deserved, due to my past betrayals or deceptions of others; it was something I had not forgiven.

The First Appearances of the Masters

After the near-death experience, I wanted to recreate the love, joy and bliss experienced during my union with Source. I asked many fundamentalist ministers, relating to them some of my experiences, and was told that it was the devil in disguise. One told me I could not enter heaven unless baptized by him, and only him.

I was tired of hearing the "You have to accept Jesus Christ as your lord and savior" and the same old wrathful God and tormenting devil routines. I told one minister that if he knew God, he would know me, and what happened to me. I also told him, "Isn't it wonderful to know we are all going to heaven, despite your judgments and condemnations?"

I was not religious when I had my NDE; I was driving a fast car and chasing fast women, but at least I was honest, cared about and was helpful to others. Overall I felt good about myself. If I made it to heaven, surely most everyone could.

I started going to Unity churches, which were much more liberal and understanding. They spoke of an all-loving, forgiving God, which was more aligned with my experience. I was also being taught from within.

Many times at night and in my meditations, a brilliant being appeared to me and showed me visions. I asked if he was the Christ, and a bolt of energy moved through my entire body. His light was so brilliant I could not clearly make out his physical appearance, though I felt his love and compassion. I did not want to talk to anyone else but Jesus. To me everyone else was a spook.

What I realized was that this was Jesus on another level, a higher level of awareness. He told me he manifests to people according to their consciousness. They create him according to their understandings, which is why there are so many images.

He taught me the true meaning of his life in a way that was very simple to understand. It was much different than that taught by most fundamentalist churches. He told me he stood for infinite love, compassion and forgiveness—attributes of the Father. He told me he was the ideal for all to find within themselves. If it were not for the back injury, I would not have taken the time to be still and know God.

The inner teachings continued until one day he appeared with a yogi whom he called Baba Ji, the Yogi Christ. I agreed to take instruction from him for a while, and was inspired by Jesus to start my studies in Eastern thought.

I found that, though Christian teachings did offer understandings, they lacked tools and techniques. Among these are deep meditation techniques and prayers designed to call forward the God within, rather than the prayer of a poor wretched sinner unworthy of becoming one with God, which was the belief taught by most fundamentalists. I had to learn about subtle energies, and understandings about the energy centers of the body that were not revealed by Christian teachings. I knew I needed to find a good yoga teacher to supplement my inner teachings.

My Introduction to Yoga

I found a wonderful yoga teacher named Clara. I told her of my condition, and she assured me we could heal it through yoga. I was getting stronger and stronger, day by day, and now could walk around for a while, though my time on my feet was limited. My right leg had still not regained full function and was now considerably shorter than my left, which did most of the walking.

The yoga class was called Bhakti yoga, and it was very balanced. We began with a unifying meditation. Clara asked us to feel what was going on inside of us, and put it into one word, if possible. What was interesting was that most of the class came up with the same word.

It seems there are group lessons in the collective consciousness. We were given a chance to talk about it, process a little, and then she started in with Hatha yoga and the postures. By the end of the class, our problems, as well as our little aches and pains, were gone. We ended in a blissful meditation.

My back was getting stronger and stronger, and it seemed as if some divine intervention was at play. One day in meditation, yogis appeared to me and I described them. Clara told me they were in the lineage of her teachers. I spent many years in her classes, along with going to every process-oriented workshop and therapy session I could find. I knew that the only thing that separated us from God was our wounds, traumas and wrong conclusions from past experiences—our beliefs. Finding ways of healing and processing were first priority to me. Several other physical yogis visited and initiated me into their forms of meditation and yoga.

A Manifesting Ceremony

One of the most impacting ceremonies we performed during the yoga classes was a manifesting ceremony. We were instructed to write down three things that were important to us, things we really desired. It was made very clear that we could not ask for world peace or something vague. It had to be things we personally desired.

I contemplated what I wanted and wrote down each

desire on a yellow piece of paper. Once everyone had written down what they wanted, an abalone shell filled with burning sage was passed around. We had to read each desire aloud and wave the burning sage into our own energy fields. We then created a fantasy around each desire and lived it as if it already existed. A prayer was said and it was released to the universe.

I asked for my house to sell; it had been on the market for over a year. I was very specific, and stated that I wanted full price and that the buyer would want to move in immediately. My second desire was for a motorcycle. The third was for a beautiful woman to come into my life.

Two days after the ceremony I received a call concerning my house. A buyer offered full price and wanted to move in immediately.

The following weekend I was given a motorcycle, a small Honda 250. I was given another motorcycle later. Both were wrecks, but just getting them was a lesson in itself: I had to be more specific.

The following week I met a beautiful woman and we started dating. We were completely incompatible, but she was strikingly beautiful. I found I needed to be a lot more specific in this arena as well, and definitely not so shallow as to focus primarily on outer appearances.

Having the three manifestations appear really boosted my faith, and I learned a lot about myself. The next time I will ask for a new baby blue Harley Sportster and a beautiful spiritually, mentally, emotionally and physically compatible life mate.

The Tibetan Foundation and Cazekiel

I met a man named Tom Dongo, who was with the Tibetan Foundation. He had incredible clairvoyant abilities. There was a strong brotherly (most likely a past-life) connection, and I invited him to live with me. We worked together, holding guided meditations and channeling classes.

My house had become a retreat center, sponsoring many different teachers, healers and authors, and I was taught many Tibetan techniques for opening to Spirit.

One day in class I was shot straight out of my body; it was like the NDE all over again. The love, joy and bliss were beyond words. People in the class were asking me to speak, and all I could say was "No words. No words can describe this." Tears were streaming down my face.

I was again in the golden white light, the plane of bliss. There, I saw a beautiful golden being appear. He had long golden hair and a golden beard that flowed into golden robes. He leaned forward, stroking his beard, and smiled an all-knowing smile. It was very humbling.

By his left hand side was what looked like a white marble stand, and there upon the stand was a book; I was to write that book. On his right side was a golden bow with golden arrows. I was told they were to be used to send the love and joy to its designated mark for healing. He said he was Cazekiel. When I returned to my body it took me two weeks to adjust back to the Earth plane.

Later in the same session an archangel was being channeled and I asked who Cazekiel is. He said, "We refer to him as the God of Eternal Bliss."

I asked the archangel, "What is my relationship to Cazekiel?"

He said, "You are his hands and feet, a teacher for the God of Eternal Bliss." He also told me I was here to work on basic interpersonal relationships. I had done too many isolated spiritual cave experiences. Cave is easy. The last thing he told me was that I would be teaching the teachers. I found myself feeling unworthy in this regard, because at the time I did not know my purpose or myself.

From that day on, I started writing the books; it was after deep meditation that I would begin to write. The words that flowed through me showed a much higher wisdom and intelligence than my own. I was shown many visions and given prophecies that would then begin to unfold with remarkable accuracy. I spent many hours learning from Masters within the Tibetan Foundation such as Djwhal Khul, Vywamus and others.

One of my first attempts at channeling was for a man who asked me to channel for him. I knew nothing of his past. A master's spirit came into me and filled my body with a warm fatherly glow. I felt very centered, and the love was pouring through me. The words came forward after a little resistance.

The Master channeling through me told the man he had to forgive his father; the Master would be the father he'd never had, if the man would allow it. The man burst into tears, and a great lifting occurred. There was more detailed information given later.

When finished, I saw the profound effect this had had on the man. What was said did not make a lot of sense to me, for I had no pre-knowledge of the man's past. I just had to trust in the message and get out of the way. Later, I was certified as a conscious channel of the highest consciousness and energy by the Tibetan Foundation.

Soul Traveling to Inner Earth

One of my most profound experiences was being taught to soul travel. We would leave in groups, creating a merkaba vehicle, and travel to other planes, dimensions and spiritual mystery centers of the Earth.

One evening we decided to go to the Great Pyramid. We found ourselves descending underneath the right paw of the Sphinx. There was a tunnel underneath the Sphinx, with adjacent rooms. As I walked down the tunnel, I looked into the rooms, seeing large clay pots, small on the bottom and larger at the top, with lids. I could see inside them and I intuitively knew they were filled with scrolls of ancient knowledge, scrolls with the knowledge of light and sound which, I was told later, was Atlantean.

I tried to enter a room, and a strange force pushed me back. The feeling I experienced was a clear message that it was not time; any further intrusion might lead to serious consequences. There was some form of guardian there to insure the knowledge was not released before its proper time. I did not argue, and went on my way down the tunnel, peeking into the other rooms. I was laughing, saying to myself, "Boy, are people going be surprised when this gets out."

I heard Tom's voice calling us back, and I returned to the room. We then wrote down what we had seen during our soul travels, and the congruency was amazing. There was no prompting, only a journey to the Sphinx and descending beneath it. All the rest we viewed on our own.

A week later we wanted to do it again. I said I wanted to go down the tunnel. We went through the same protocols and the next thing I knew I was with my spiritual partners in the tunnel, moving down a very long, winding path with torches along the way. It was as if someone knew we were coming.

We came to a great wooden door with very large metallic rings for handles. The door opened, and on the other side was a very small man who looked elfin. Despite his short size, he had immense power and authority. On either side of him were very tall beings that were eight to ten feet high. It was obvious that the smaller gentleman was in charge, due to his spiritual advancement. He greeted us with a warm all-knowing smile, and turned for us to follow him. We walked down many paths.

On one path there were jungles, various terrains and all sorts of animals; even mythological ones we believe are extinct had been preserved. We felt no fear, because the people had telepathic control over the animals and there seemed to be a mutual respect.

One path had large domed crystalline or glass structures on it. Large main domes were connected to smaller personal domes, and they all fit into the landscape, with paths through lush flora. There were spacecraft hovering about, and some looked more like pure brilliant orange and gold plasma energy than metallic ships.

As we went further, we came to what looked like a great sea or lake. On the beach, neatly stacked, were planes and boats of various sizes, and I was told that they were from the Bermuda Triangle. Most of the passengers were living within the Earth's interior now. They had the choice to leave, but when given the opportunity to experience the interior, they chose to stay.

We could see a few of them walking about with blissful grins on their faces. I was told they had been caught up in the opening of a great door, a swirling G-force that created a vortex, allowing access in and out of the interior. We were told that there were many survivors from the days of Atlantis and Lemuria who had ventured inwards during the cataclysms.

When we finished our tour, the small man revealed his name to me. He said, "I am Debeg. I am an ambassador for the Inner Earth. We are showing you this because we are very concerned.

We share the waters and the air with those on the surface. We are also very worried about your underground nuclear testing, which is an explosion in our heavens. You are fracturing the Earth's crust. Every blast will be met with a reaction and release, felt by you as earthquakes. You are not only jeopardizing yourselves, you are jeopardizing us as well, by poisoning the air and water and by nuclear testing. This must stop."

He was dead serious and I felt the intensity of his words. He turned and left and we were told it was time to go. We followed the same path up the tunnel and back to the room.

When we returned, Tom said, "Okay, write down what you saw." We did, and again the similarities down to minute details were amazing. I have always been open-minded, but I dismissed the experience as group hallucination or mental telepathy or someone else's imagination. Surely this was too wild to be real.

Another OBE with Cazekiel

The second time I engaged Cazekiel was in a meditation class. Our group was meditating together and the whole room began to fill with golden light; everyone could feel it. I had been having several problems, the usual everyday-life kind, and all of a sudden, again I was propelled out of my body. I kept expanding into ever more ecstatic states of love and bliss. I looked back at the Earth, and it was the size of a grain of sand. Cazekiel said to me, "There, back there are your problems. This is who you really are."

From that expanded awareness, my problems became so small they were imperceptible. Even the Earth was barely visible, and so far away. I came back into my body again and felt much lighter.

I then really had trouble for a few days in grounding myself. Everything had a shimmering light around it, even the trash on the beach that used to upset me due to the inconsiderate nature of those who had left it. I could now see that the trash was made of the same God substance as everything else. I could not even judge the trash.

The Teaching of the Inner Christ

I found a new spiritual system called the Teaching of the Inner Christ, which was a blend of East and West, minus the dogma. I loved it, for it was full of the techniques and understandings I needed to further my spiritual path. It also offered a firm foundation that later I found to be a little too firm. Then I discovered I was battling with unseen negative influences that would come to me like a moth to a flame.

One night I was in a fight for my life. There was a dark, ominous entity that was trying to take over my body. I awoke and could not get back fully into the physical. The more I tried, the harder this thing fought me. I had regained partial consciousness and was trying to move my body but did not have much control yet. I claimed, "I AM THE LIVING CHRIST." I called out to Jesus, Baba Ji and the Source Itself for help.

Little by little I began to regain control. I stood up and started walking, and with each step I claimed, "I AM." I mustered up all the courage and self-authority I could, while walking around the room. I decided to go outside and walk down to the beach; all the while, this thing kept trying to take over. It was almost sunrise, and at last I had complete control of my body. Once the sun rose, I felt I had won. The presence was gone.

As I sat on the beach, I was angry that this could occur. I asked the Masters why they would let this happen; I thought I had protection. The reply was, "It is necessary that you experience some things as part of your teachings. Just telling you there are possessing entities, discarnate spirits, etc., is not enough. It was part of your training and initiation. You did well."

I was really struggling with what was happening to me. I am a very down-to-earth, practical kind of guy. I told the Masters, "If you want me to continue, I need solid proof that this is real. Not just a runaway imagination."

Where I sat on the beach there were no rocks or shells, just sand. When I opened my eyes, there right in front of me was a rock. It was a perfect heart. My mind still would not totally accept the manifestation. I told myself there was still the possibility that I did not see it before. I figured that a wave had uncovered it, even though it was obviously above the watermark.

I went home, rock in hand, and showed it to Tom, without any explanation. He said, "Nice manifestation. Jesus created that for you. You needed solid proof." I have the rock to this day as a reminder to stay the course.

The T.I.C. was a great class. I had many breakthroughs there, learned invaluable tools and techniques, and furthered my contact with the Masters.

One day Jesus came to me in class. The leader of the group asked me to speak. I refused at first, and the energy kept building. I knew I had to release it. The words came forward: "The universe is like one big puzzle; it is all God, and it is all coming together."

I was told the ETs were of different origins and their bodies are adaptations to their environments. They have different agendas, some benevolent, serving the Creator; some in need, serving themselves.

I was informed by the minister that ETs were not part of the T.I.C. program, and advised not to go in that direction, for it was not welcome. I knew it needed to be addressed, and decided I had to find a more open forum. Jesus opened my mind to the possibility of spiritually and technologically advanced ETs. I had to find the answers. The censorship of messages from ETs has since lessened within the T.I.C. due to the constant contact experiences had by many of their students and teachers.

Initiations and Spiritual Power Feedings

There were several events in my life which I have turned over to the Great Mystery. I may never know what transpired, yet flowing with the event is often more important.

I decided early one Sunday morning to go to church. There was a wonderful Unity Church in Santa Cruz, California. The minister's name was Emily, and her sermons were usually right on the mark concerning the times people everywhere were experiencing.

I met a woman there named Christie. There was an instant spiritual connection. We sat together during the talk and Christie grabbed my hand. I turned to look at her and she was fully illuminated. She was starting to fear the experience, and became disoriented. I told her to let go, and release the energy to the audience.

She was experiencing a direct transmission from Spirit.

It was a power feeding, and she was an anchor or transmitter for the entire gathering. I told her she was safe...the only danger was not trusting...blocking the flow of spiritual energies. She squeezed my hand and relaxed, allowing the transmission to dispense throughout the audience.

I began to hear sighing all around me. People were clearly receiving the dispensation. Many commented on how they felt. Some felt lifted, lighter and at peace. Some felt an overwhelming love settle upon them.

When the service was over, Christie could not move. She could not get up out of her chair. I had to help her ground the energy, bring it down through her feet into the earth. Finally she could stand again. She said she felt like Bambi with wobbly legs. She also was transformed, elevated to a much higher level of consciousness. She said many of her problems were gone and seemed to be erased. She was also very clear she had a higher purpose that needed her attention.

Christie would stop into the import shop where I worked from time to time to get feedback on some of her decisions. I would just smile and say, "That feels really good, how does it feel to you?"

She would smile back and say, "I already knew the answer, just needed the reflection."

There was another event that happened in a restaurant in Eugene, Oregon. I was having breakfast, and a man walked by my table. He stopped for a moment and had that blank look in his face. A voice inside me said, "He is going down." I jumped up and caught him just in the nick of time. I grabbed his shirt with one hand and the back of his head with the other and laid him down. There was a waiter who helped me.

With my left hand on the back of his head and my right hand on his heart, I pulled from Spirit all the energy I could muster. I was told he would be fine. It was his time. I realized it was not an illness, a stroke or heart attack. It was an initiation. His soul knew this was the perfect opportunity, and laid him down for the experience. There has to be an absence of ego for this to happen, an altered state of consciousness where the ego or conscious mind is not present to block the reunion of the higher self. He had been asking for such an event, only it came on spirit's time, not his.

The waitresses were calling 911, and I told them he would be fine. Just then his eyes opened and he sat up with that "Where was I?" look on his face.

I picked up the phone and asked the questions they required. "Do you have a history of losing consciousness, are you diabetic, is there a history of heart problems or stroke?"

He said, "No, I am in perfect health. I am fine, and just need to go to my office and make sense of all this." He had to assimilate the experience, and one look at his face showed a clear transformation. He stood up and walked off, normal as could be.

The waiters and waitresses were shocked. They had no reference points for what had happened. I said, "That was interesting." I smiled and went back to my table and finished my breakfast.

One of the waiters came to me and said, "What happened? That did not make sense."

I just smiled and said, "No, it doesn't, on this level."

I experienced these events on a regular basis once I began counseling others. We would clear out old wounds, traumas and wrong conclusions from past experience, and when enough boulders were cleared, the river of spirit would rush in, creating love, joy and ecstatic bliss. A renewed sense of well-being and clarity of purpose often followed the counseling.

The Visions

I was having visions on a regular basis, and I would see personal events before they unfolded. I would also see many Earth changes that were coming in the future. Some of them were very upsetting, because I knew they impacted friends and family. They also threatened my own security, for I was living right on the coast. I had to learn how to view them without attachment.

I also began to have visions of a large mountain with a river on its eastern border, and behind a certain parcel of land was a little mountain. I did not know where it was. I found a map of the United States and used a pendulum to divine the location of the property seen in the vision. The pendulum started spinning wildly over Mt. Adams in Western Washington; my hand became really hot over the area as well.

After the vision, I knew I was to create a learning and healing retreat center in Washington, because we were so overcrowded and needed more land and a bigger meeting room. My house in Santa Cruz was jam-packed with people coming to the meditations and channeling classes.

I was also seeing visions of the West Coast being hit by massive quakes and tsunamis in the distant future. I was told there would be a large quake in the near future, hitting our area in Northern California. I gave people the location, magnitude and time of the event; it hit right on schedule.

Before the quake hit, I was chastised and told I was creating gloom and doom, and even that I was attracting the quake. Many groups rose up to condemn the information and me. I tried to warn as many people as possible, only to push their denial, attachment and survival issues to the surface.

There was lots of damage when the Loma-Prieta/San Francisco quake hit. In the old mall, brick buildings went down, people were trapped, and even killed. The new mall lost its roof, homes suffered severe damage, and some slid down the mountainside they were perched upon. I saw in the news one of the major freeways collapsed. Overpasses came down with unsuspecting drivers, one of which was a motorcycle cop, which found themselves airborne.

What was sad was that even after the event, they were still angry. One would think there would be a little humility.

I wanted to return and teach more classes, yet some of my best friends had turned their backs on me, holding a grudge. I saw it as a message to fully devote my attention to the retreat center.

Sri Yukteswar and the Pajamas

The chastisement I'd been continuously undergoing left an element of doubt in my mind. To have so many people rise up against one, receiving very little support, begins to wear on the individual. I started to understand the meaning of the words "A Christ has no place to rest his head." I saw how the teachings that had the greatest followings were the ones that do not challenge the ego or separate self. The teachings that did not upset the status quo and allowed the people to continue in denial were the most popular.

Social consciousness is based on separation. It is a paradox; people gather together, agree, and then go live a life of separation. They live as if they are separate from each other and from life, miss the truth of omnipresence, and do not see the Creator in all Creation. This accepted concept of separation allows them to do as they wish to others and nature, often becoming willing participants in actions that are not in the highest and best good for humanity and the Earth.

If one were to use impeccable integrity and choose to eliminate most of the jobs that did not serve humanity and the Earth, jobs that "leeched" off the creative energies and labors of others rather than producing something of value, or if one eliminated jobs that were harmful in one way or another to humanity and the Earth, we would have over 70 percent unemployment. Yet the same people gather in religious and spiritual groups, professing their love for humanity and the Earth. Some are even worshipped or admired for the great wealth they have amassed at the expense of humanity and the Earth.

I could not understand the hypocrisy of going to church

or other spiritual functions on the weekend and dismissing the Creator from Creation all during the week. Many would spend all week destroying or harming nature so that they could go out on the weekend and enjoy it. The quest for union with God or Spirit seemed to deny physicality, and many Old Age and New Age teachings dismissed physicality altogether as the illusion of something other than God.

Here is a little eye-opener: What good is gaining the world and losing one's soul? What good is destroying the very platform for life in our quest for security? What good is having all the toys and no planet, or a planet that is not conducive to life?

The last and most important thing to contemplate is that what we do here in the physical has a direct impact on our spirit or soul, and it determines where we go in our next understanding. This very message has had me thrown out of some of the most "holy" of churches. Why? It was because their existence or very survival was determined by the donations of men and women who made their money at the expense of others. To them, I was a grim reminder and, heavens forbid, we cannot upset our biggest donors.

I was becoming very frustrated; beginning to think there was something wrong with me. I surrendered to a deep meditation to release my frustrations, asking for help, when a man with the regal face of a lion appeared to me. There was a brilliant light around him, and he told me to stay the course. He also said I was a man of integrity, which is currently hard to find, and he made it very clear that I was not to define self by the opinions of others.

I drifted off to sleep after the meditation and awoke refreshed with new charge and vigor. I had seen a picture of Sri Yukteswar before (Paramahansa Yogananda's guru), and knew it was him.

My first thought after waking up was that I needed a pair of pajamas. We often had visitors staying overnight on the sofas; I slept in the nude, which would have made it quite uncomfortable to guests if I had to get up in the middle of the night. My second thought was, "I wonder if that was my imagination or really Yukteswar?"

An hour later, a good friend appeared at my doorstep. She had just left a channeling session conducted by a woman who was channeling none other than Sri Yukteswar. She tossed me a bag, and in it was a pair of pajamas. She said, "Yukteswar said to get these for you. He also said you were a man of high integrity—sometimes too high—and it hampers your work." A chill ran down my spine, followed by an incredible wave of energy. It was Sri Yukteswar, and I could feel him laughing in pure bliss. There was nothing I could do but to join him.

The Exodus to Washington

The exodus to Washington State happened in two stages. During the first stage, we formed a group and invited anyone who wanted to be a part of the community to come. In our first meetings many came, but each individual had a dream or a desire and felt that their way was the only way. We had every possible extreme, from survivalists who wanted to buy a military tank and build bunkers, to people who thought God would provide everything and there was nothing to worry about or do.

No matter how hard we tried, we could not create consensus on anything. I had sold my house, so two women and I decided to go out and find the property. It was the only thing we agreed on as a group.

We traveled through several states and ended up in Cle Elum, Washington, finding a very large piece of property on a river. Although it was not the same location I had divined on the map, at the time it felt right. I secured the property with a deposit, not knowing it was a process to go through, rather than the place that was meant for me.

When we returned to Santa Cruz, it was now time for a commitment. This pushed everyone's issues up. Many had to demonize us to validate their fears and break their prior commitment. I understood the process and depersonalized it, realizing that even though we did not form a community, the process was just as important. We often forget that the journey is just as important as the end destination, and evolution occurs all along the way.

A Night with Bigfoot

On our scouting journey we stopped at a little campground in the Snoqualmie mountains. We were tired, and had a Volkswagen van set up for camping. At about 2 AM we heard a loud cry and groan, sounding like something between a cat and a human. My first impression was Bigfoot; then my mind jumped in and said it was probably a bear or cougar. The women were locking doors, exhibiting sheer terror. Something inside of me told me I had to check it out, even though I was told by my companions that I was crazy to go out there after a scream like that.

It was a full-moon night and I could see very well, so down the path I went. I was prepared, however, to put my feet in reverse and hightail it back at any moment. I could still hear the moaning, so I knew where and how far away the creature was. I quietly crept down the path, keeping my ears and eyes on full alert. It seemed like all my senses were tingling.

The path opened up to a beach on a lake, and next to the lake was a large fallen tree stump, with a small bush in front of it. A large dark figure was sitting on the stump. I could see clearly that it was not a bear or a cougar. It stood up in a crouched position when it sensed my presence, and stopped its groaning. I felt it was deeply hurt or saddened by something. I held my hands at my sides, palms out, and sent it all the love and compassion I could muster.

The creature stood up a little taller. I tried to get closer and when I took a step, it crouched back down; I knew it did not trust me. I was between it and the forest, and the lake was behind it. The only way out was past me, about fifty feet to my left; there was unobstructed beach in that fifty feet. We stood there, looking at each other under the full moon for about ten minutes. I tried to establish some kind of communication, telepathically sending out love and peace. I could tell it was extremely sensitive, because it was reacting to what I was sending, by relaxing and standing more upright. But it still did not want to have anything to do with humans.

Finally it stood totally erect and walked right by me, less than fifty feet away. I could see it was something in between an ape and a man, more human-like in the face. The creature was very tall, and I could tell it was female because it had large breasts. It did not run away, but walked very slowly, upright, eyes fixed upon me the whole time. All I sensed was that it wanted to be left alone.

When I returned home, Tom said he had been doing some remote viewing of our trip. I told him something had happened in the mountains when we camped. He smiled and said, "Bigfoot." There is no way that he could have known, because we had just arrived home, and nobody had called ahead.

Tom told me it was a female, and that she was upset because she had lost her daughter. That is why I got so close to her; she was distraught. This all checked out with the experience. I asked him if he could look into it further and see if she had found her daughter. He said, "Her daughter is with the others; they found her and all is well."

The women and I also saw some strange lights that night in the forest, moving very fast and maneuvering around trees and rocks as if some intelligence were guiding them. I believe the Bigfoot are the overseers of the nature kingdom. They have the ability to shift in and out of dimensions or shape-shift, and are very advanced in the nature kingdom rather than in the technological, or what we mistakenly call the civilized, kingdom.

Bigfoot are part of the human experience that took a

different path in evolution. The interaction with the female Bigfoot changed my life. With one glance from her, there was more understanding conveyed than I have ever had with humans. It was as if she communicated telepathically in whole sentences that came as feelings.

Strange Happenings on the Road

While on the road, one of my traveling companions asked me if I wanted to try a spiritual experiment. It was a technique for accessing past lives. I was game, and she lit a candle, then put it in front of us. We began to stare at each other in a relaxed fashion. As we stared, she transformed into a large, very menacing Viking warrior. His face was smudged with the smoke and ash from a campfire. He was very tall and muscular and, to be frank, it scared the crap out of me. I jerked back and the apparition vanished.

I told her what I had seen and that of course it was her past life, definitely not mine. As I sat there, I began to feel a deep sadness and to get mental pictures of the Viking's life. He was a merciless warrior, yet I understood what had made him that way. The images showed me how he had lost his family, who were brutally murdered. I had to embrace him and heal the wounds and traumas, for he was a part of me. It was one of my own past lives, my own inner wounded warrior, and I needed his strength and courage for the next adventure. After healing and embracing the Viking warrior and reclaiming his unique aspects or gifts back into my inner arsenal, we continued on our journey.

I noticed that, as evidenced by strong impressions and sensations, we were not alone on this journey. There were Masters and angelic guides with us. We had a heightened sensitivity during the trip; this was both a blessing and a curse. Whenever we entered small towns, we felt the entire consciousness of the people there. We had to do a lot of clearing work just to maintain our sanity. We would actually get headaches when coming into these towns, and they would leave as soon as we passed through—one of the many lessons that come with expanded consciousness.

One event in particular was when we stopped in Mt. Shasta. We were walking down the main street and I saw a woman coming toward us. She had a blank look on her face, and there was an energy around her that was not right. I intuitively crossed the street, asking the other two women to come with me. They started to, but one turned back because she knew the woman. She ran over to her and gave her a big hug, telling her how great it was to see her. The woman showed little emotion, barely acknowledged my friend and went on her way.

Shortly afterward, my friend was in complete disarray, as if something had possessed her and hooked into her energies. She was lying down in the camper with nausea, feeling very ill. I was guided to turn around and use my right hand to channel energy to her with the intent of removing the other energies. My hand heated up and a flow of healing energies came rushing through from me to her. The negative energies were dispelled, and she was immediately well. I never knew I could do that; I just followed the intuition to hold up my hand.

We decided after that to go up to the mountaintop and spend the day. In one of my meditations up there, I saw a robed priest who was bigger than the mountain itself. The vision was very humbling. There were many other experiences on the mountain, yet this was the most profound.

One thing I will never forget, during another trip to Shasta that soon followed, was the appearance of a woman all dressed in white robes or a flowing gown. I was coming down off the mountain when she crossed below me in front of our group. She stopped and held her arms up to them, and it seemed as if she was addressing them. She was there for a while and then continued down the mountain, disappearing behind a rock. She never came out the other side and seemed to vanish into thin air.

I asked the group what the woman had said to them. They said, "What woman?" They were all facing her and had to see her, yet not one saw her. I found out later about the race of beings that were tall and blonde, living inside the mountain. It appears she was one of them.

Successful Attempt for Washington

The second attempt for Washington was more successful. Having dealt with all the fickle emotions and indecisions of the group energy, I realized I had to follow my own inner guidance and not rely on others. The owners of the Cle Elum land called me and said, "We want more money for the land," after having already agreed on a price.

I asked them, "Does this mean you are not accepting my original offer?" They said yes and I said, "Great. I will expect my deposit back in three days." Thank God they too were fickle and indecisive, because I was not meant to live there. The universe works in strange ways. I was offered a job in Hood River, Oregon. It is just 30 minutes from Mt. Adams, which, as I had received in earlier guidance, was the place for me. It felt right, and I packed my bags, heading off for Hood River.

I found a real estate agent and told him I wanted to be near Mt. Adams. He showed me all over Hood River, and very little on the Washington side. I repeatedly told him my spirit was guiding me over to the Washington side, and Oregon did not feel right.

One day while on the Washington side, I saw a sign that made a chill run down my spine. I knew that I was to contact that other agency. I struggled with it, because the first agent had shown me property and spent time with me, yet was not doing what I wanted. I heard within, "To thine own self be true; follow Spirit."

I called the number on the sign, talked to a man and explained what I wanted. He said, "I know exactly what you are looking for." I scheduled an appointment and he took me to a couple of other properties. I walked out on the land and said, "No, this is not it." He said, "I wanted to show you something comparable first," and then he took me to my spot. The ranch was not even for sale, but there was a divorce underway and he knew the owners.

When I walked out on the land, a charge of energy went through me that was undeniable. I looked up and there stood majestic Mt. Adams. It had a large lenticular cloud that was bright orange underneath. It changed form and billowed up, looking like a scene from the Old Testament. I looked above me and a lone bald eagle was circling. To the east was the White Salmon River and behind me, incredibly enough, was a small mountain called Little Mountain—exactly like the visions. I turned to the agent and said, "I believe this is it."

On my following birthday, two more signs appeared. When I awoke, a bald eagle was sitting in the tree right outside my window. I was on the second story staring right at it when I opened my eyes. It seemed as if he was staring back intently. I thanked him; he seemed to nod his head and took to the air.

Later that day I was out watering the garden, and a shadow was circling me on the ground. I looked up, and what looked like a pure white hawk, a little smaller than the eagle, was circling overhead. I watched it for a while, trying to identify it. It was not like any other hawk or falcon I had ever seen. Having raised hawks and falcons, I was very aware of the different species.

I turned my eyes to the ground for a second because it went into the sun. What was odd was that there was no shadow on the ground—it vanished instantaneously. I looked up again with a full 360 degrees of vision, and there was nothing in the sky. It seemed to have just vanished. There is always the possibility of a dive on some unsuspecting prey, yet I could not come up with an acceptable answer for the almost instant disappearance. My Native American friends, of course, had the answer.

Back at the Ranch

I purchased the land and moved to Hood River, Oregon. My sister had rented a house there, and I moved into one of the rooms. It was just half an hour from the ranch and had heat, water, etc.

I had met a new girlfriend, and she was on a spiritual quest as well. She had also had an NDE, and was what many refer to as a walk-in. When she awakened after her accident, she could no longer relate to her family or her boyfriend, and was really struggling.

Having gone through a similar experience, I understood hers, and it seemed destined by Spirit that we should be together. She and I worked in the store with my sister part-time, and I spent the rest of the time up at the ranch, building the center. However, her desires led her more into windsurfing, partying and a drug or two, which caused separation between us.

I remember her coming up to the ranch one day; she had been out partying all night. Her aura was gray. She had indulged in some cocaine as well and joined the "see me, dig me" crowd. The spiritual quest gave way to the lower nature, the party nature, and we continued to grow apart. I told her where she was going and that I could not go there. If she wanted to go for the light, she could join me. A few days later she ran off with a windsurfer and moved to Canada.

I put up a tent when spring came, next to the main building that was being erected, and I had a large wooden box for supplies. There was a creek and a small pond that became my bath for the time being.

Just being on the land completely energized me. There was an old wooden bridge on the property, out of which the previous owner had decided to build a large barn. It was 66 feet long, 21 feet wide, and in the past, fully loaded logging trucks had crossed over it on a regular basis.

The owner tried to build the barn two different times.

The first time, a storm destroyed it; the second time, heavy snow collapsed it and nature made sure he did not finish his project. I think it was due to some karma around his logging business.

I myself had a run-in with an angry gnome on the property (more about that later). There was an agreement made between us, however, and from then on, nothing happened to stop the project. In fact the project took a divine turn for the better.

We were given perfect windows that matched the angle of the beams. We framed in the bridge, put the siding on, and were starting on the roof. After applying the first third of the shingles, we ran out. I had been meditating earlier in the morning and Baba Ji told me, "Do not worry; all your needs will be met."

I had two friends named Dave and Tom helping me. They said, "We are out of shingles."

I told them, "All will be provided. Not to worry; they will be here."

Now these are carpenters and down-to-earth, discerning men. They said, "Yeah, right. He has lost it," and started wondering where we could buy some more shingles.

Just then, a truck started up the dirt road leading to the site. Lo and behold, it was full of shingles. A man stepped out and said, "I am finished building, and I have all these shingles. Do you want them?" My two friends sat there with their jaws wide open; I was grinning from ear to ear. We quickly unloaded the shingles and started in with new exuberance. We jokingly said, "We are on a mission of God," yet still did not want to fully admit it.

After the second batch of shingles was in place, we were still only two-thirds finished with the roof (the main lodge is a very big building). I had a ritual of greeting the sun with a morning meditation, and again early that morning I heard, "Do not worry; all will be provided."

It was now noon and my two friends were giving me a hard time, saying "So, oh great sage, where are the shingles?"

I laughed and said, "It is noon. Time for lunch. They will be here when they are supposed to be here."

We went to lunch ,and when we returned, another truck was sitting on the site, fully loaded with shingles. It was the same story again, for this man was also finished building and had a lot of extra shingles. It was near Christmas and he did not have any money for presents, etc. I asked him, "How much for the shingles?" He started to give them to us, but we worked out a fair price and I paid him. He was jumping up and down for joy when we parted, for now he could give his family what they wanted.

My friends and I worked through Christmas, uncovering a little of the roof at a time and laying down the shingles. We would stop every so often and light a fire in a trash can to thaw our fingers. We had finished the last of the north side and snow was blowing in our faces as we completed the south.

At last the Bridge House was buttoned up; the roof was on, the windows and siding were installed, and the doors were hung. It was a good feeling, because now we could move indoors. The first thing we installed was the wood stove. It was a must for survival. Without insulation and drywall, the building offered little more than sanctuary from frostbite.

Txosamarra

One evening I was meditating, and a wonderful presence made itself known. It was the same presence that had been with me before, when many visions of the future were coming to me, but I did not know it by name. I was struggling with its name because it was an ancient, foreign name I had never heard. I asked myself, "How come I can't just have a guide named Bob or Charlie? Why is it always these ancient characters?" The spelling of the name was very bizarre, and I had to double-check it to make sure I got it right.

After meditating for a while, getting acquainted, I decided to go inside, at my sister's house, for dinner. My sister was very worried about her children. She was divorced and had just let them go with their father on a journey from Hood River, Oregon, all the way back to Orange County, California. His car was not in great shape, and she could not stop worrying.

I told her, "After dinner, let's meditate and see what comes in." So we sat down and lit a candle. While in meditation, Txosamarra came in and the room began to fill with flashing lights. The first thing he said was, "The children are fine. They are being well taken care of."

What we did not know at the time was that her husband's car had broken down. A woman stopped and gave them a ride to her house. Her husband was a mechanic for the school buses and, together with my sister's husband, they went back for the car. They found it had a thermostat problem, drove it to the garage, and installed a new one. He did not even charge for labor. The kids were being fed in the meantime, watching their favorite movie, "Ghostbusters." All was well, and they were soon back on the road.

Txosamarra ended with a few words about who he was, in relationship to me. He said, "I am what is referred to as your Christ self in the vibrational continuum." Then he told my sister, "By the way, those flashing lights you are seeing are not the candle." He had read her mind, because just then she was thinking that the flashing lights she was seeing out the corners of her eyes were just the candle flickering.

She smiled and said, "How did he know what I was thinking?" and it gave her verification that the rest of the message was correct. She could now release the fears around her children. I spent many long hours with Txosamarra. His accuracy concerning Earth changes was impeccable.

Meeting the Ram

My sister told me about a woman up in our area named J.Z. Knight who was channeling a 35,000-year-old entity named Ramtha. There was much controversy over her work, and I had heard all kinds of stories. There was an event held in Yelm, Washington, in a large barn where Ramtha would speak to the audience. I already felt very comfortable with my own inner guidance, yet when my sister acquired some tickets to the event, I decided to go.

A few days earlier I had decided to go to a small hill surrounded by trees facing the mountain, where I often meditated. It was a special place, for I had many incredible awakenings there. I began watching my breath, going into deep meditation, and a curious wind seemed to come from nowhere. I felt a very strong presence, and there was thought-to-thought communication. I said, "If you truly are the Ram, I know you are omnipresent and you can hear my words. I want the following three questions to be answered."

My sister came and picked me up later that week, and we were off to Yelm. Little did I know that when I entered the barn, there would be about 500 people inside. When J.Z. Knight walked out on stage, Ramtha had already entered her body. She was in full trance, and he marched across the stage in a very determined manner. He turned and addressed my three questions. He further elaborated on them and gave a wonderful dissertation on the seven levels of man. I was deeply honored that, with such a large audience, he would be taking the time to address my personal questions.

Then I began to wonder, which came first, the chicken or the egg? Was that event already set up, along with the topics, and I was led to it, or was he addressing me specifically? The questions were specific and very diverse, and were answered in order. One question in particular concerned the use of drugs, and worshipping of the body rather than living according to thc spirit within thc body. It was a last-ditch effort to heal my relationship and my girlfriend, who accompanied us. Unfortunately for her, the Ram's words fell on deaf ears.

One thing I do remember is that he said you couldn't instill want into another. He pointed directly at me and said,

"Master, I will take away that which is not bringing you joy." My girlfriend left two days later. During the lecture, Ramtha told us to "go out into nature and I will show you how greatly you are loved."

I had planned a trip to Mt. Shasta, and there he made good on his promise. I was on the bank of Lake Siskiyou for an evening meditation, when a strange breeze came up out of nowhere, along with a wonderful feeling. It stopped as soon as it started. I asked within, "Okay, blow again," and it would start, and then stop. I would wait for quite a while and there was still no wind, so I'd say, "Okay, blow again," and sure enough, it blew again. This went on for a while, and soon I had to admit that the wind was intelligent, and it was probably the Ram.

Just then a very large trout jumped right in front of me, bringing me back to physical awareness. There were birds everywhere near the place I was sitting, singing away, that had not been there before. A squirrel hopped up on my knee and put his little paws on my chest and looked right into my eyes, with no fear. I heard a rustling behind me and two deer were standing a couple of feet away. It was like a Bambi movie. The joy and bliss I felt were overwhelming. I was very grateful for the experience. Nonetheless, it continued to haunt me, and I knew I was not finished with the Ram.

Just Me and the Coyotes

The inside of the Bridge House was primarily finished without help. I could not afford to continue paying my other two friends, and after giving them a bonus and heartfelt thanks, one went back to Santa Cruz and the other quickly found another job.

I was out digging the holes for the decks on the south side and I kept hitting rock. I needed a breaker bar to open up the holes, because a post-hole digger and shovel would not break through. I meditated on where I could find such a tool. I figured Spirit would guide me to a garage sale where I would find just the right tool, since I was on a really tight budget. I was told, "Keep digging."

I said, "This is crazy. I cannot get through the rock." I decided to try another hole and see if I could get through without hitting rock. I thrust the shovel into the ground and heard a metallic clang. The impact stung my hands. I started uncovering the metallic object, and lo and behold, there was a perfect breaker bar! It was a six-foot-long, heavy iron bar and had a wedge-shaped tip. Perfect!

While working on my own, I developed a schedule where I would greet the sun with a morning meditation, and then go to breakfast completely blissed out. The locals would look at me, thinking, "He is on drugs. No one is that happy and alert in the morning, especially without a few cups of coffee." When I sat down to breakfast, I met many of the locals. Many could not understand the bliss I was experiencing, and had to invalidate it. When I talked to some of them, they thought I was stoned.

I remembered my own redneck days earlier, before the NDE, and thought of how I would have reacted. I used to view the tree-huggers and airy-fairies (which is what we called them back then) and think they were either nuts or avoiding the duties and responsibilities of life. I was more of a cowboy and carpenter back then, and maintaining my manly stature was first priority.

After the NDE, all of that seemed to wash away. I was more balanced and open afterwards, with a deep love for humanity and nature. I realized I had to tone myself down when going into town—when in Rome, do as the Romans do.

One of the things I remembered most during those times was the coyotes. They would circle around the Bridge House at night, serenading with their short yaps and chilling howls. I felt it was a welcoming party, but a part of me wondered if I was going to be their dinner. However, I knew from my days of growing up in the desert that they were harmless, so I decided to sneak out and stalk them, staff in hand. It was eerie to be out in the middle of a field with them yapping all around me, never seeing them but knowing I was surrounded.

Early Spiritual Gatherings

The first gatherings were small. People had heard of this crazy mystic who was building what looked like a large wooden ark out in the middle of a field. The Bridge House was appropriately named, because it was built out of a bridge and it was for the spiritual purposes of bridging the gap of separation. I knew my purpose was focused on universal peace, brotherly/sisterly love, equality and individual freedom for all. The vision was to create a place where all cultures and faiths could come together and share the universal principles and understandings found in all religions—common ground where the similarities were focused on, rather than the differences.

I thought that once people knew of my mission, they would jump in and help, realizing the value of such an undertaking. After all, a center that focused on universal peace, where everyone was welcomed, should be well received. I was in for a rude awakening. It was like a field of dreams. I felt inside that if I built it, they would come. Later, I wondered if what they really said was, "If you build it, you are dumb."

I posted flyers welcoming people to come for world and personal healing meditations, stating our goals and intentions. Very few came. The ones who did come often wanted a free handout. I found myself spending most of my time ministering to their needs and ignoring my own needs, as well as the needs of the center. I kept giving, hoping that they would learn by example.

One day, after being completely drained on all levels, I went up into the mountains and asked, "Why? Why do they not give, or value what is given? I am doing all I can to teach by example, but they just take."

I was told, "It is because you do not value your work." I was also told that I had many past-life vows of poverty in dedicated service to God, but that God did not want to see me living in poverty.

I knew it would take time to heal these wrong conclusions from past experiences, and they plague me to this day. I also realized I was projecting my own giving nature on others. I could not expect them to feel the same devotion and commitment I did, for they had not had the same reunion with Source. I have also seen how churches demand tithing, capitalizing on the fear of losing God's favor, and on feelings of unworthiness and guilt. I vowed never to fall into that trap. I would rather lose everything and keep my integrity.

What was sad was that I found myself between a rock and a hard place. Many Christians were quick to judge and condemn me because I did not support their wrathful images of God, or devils to blame as scapegoats for people's choices and self-created realities. Instead, we at the center taught people to take responsibility and hold themselves accountable for their attitudes, emotions and actions. This was in accordance with the teachings of Jesus when he said, "As you believe, so it is," and "As you sow, so shall you reap." It was the basic law of karma.

Even Buddha said, "We are what we think; all that we are, arises in our thoughts, and with our thoughts we create the world." He also said, "A fool and his mischief are like fresh milk; as surely as the cart follows the horse that carries it, it will catch up."

We also taught people that men and women are created in the same image and likeness of God. The light that lighteth every man and woman is the light of God. The temple is within, and once you transcend the body and the personality, you are spirit. The spark can expand to become the full flame. This was the most blasphemous to fundamentalists, who depend upon the false belief in separation holding man and woman far from God, with the ministers of course as the go-between.

Jesus often revealed his true teachings from within, along with the meaning of his life, which in many cases was completely distorted by kings and religions to fit their needs. Although it still remains written in the Bible, few Christians or ministers understand it, for they are passing down what was passed down to them in error. We continued to teach deep meditation techniques, and Intuitional and Inner Sensitivity Training, as well as yoga, but we were very remotely located and the students were few.

The True Teachings of Jesus

To fully understand the true teachings of Jesus, one must look at the sequence of events in his life. In the beginning he was born of man/woman. He said, "I am the son of man."

Later in his sojourn he began to receive messages from within. He realized he was a messenger of God and said, "I am a messenger of God."

Further into his life's work he said, "I am the son of God," for he transcended the body and the personality into the world of spirit, knowing now he was a spirit born of Spirit. For this, they took up stones and tried to kill him.

In his last days he said, "I AM GOD." He experienced total immersion with GOD and became one with GOD. He said, "I of myself do nothing, the Father through me doeth the works."

He also said, "Ye are Gods and ye will do greater works than these, for I go on to the Father." Jesus was the exemplar Christ—the example of the Christ Consciousness within all of us, a path that all must eventually follow. The Christ Consciousness is when man/woman knows themselves to be GOD, and GOD knows self to be man/woman—a union of the two into one.

The greatest misperception which has caused separation, division, war and the death of millions is the belief that the man and the personality Jesus is the way, the truth and the light, and no one shall enter heaven but through him. It was GOD speaking through Jesus, and that same GOD spoke through other master teachers throughout various cultures.

Judging, condemning and warring over names, images and doctrines was never the path of Jesus. It is the path of those who desire to enslave, control and manipulate the masses for power, position and wealth. Jesus stood for infinite love, compassion and forgiveness. There are those who serve GOD and those who serve religious institutions; you will know them by their deeds.

After experiencing the true nature of Jesus and the love and compassion of other great Masters, I cringe at what is being taught in many fundamentalist churches. It is truly anti- the Christ Consciousness, for there is no room for fear, guilt and unworthiness in the heavens. These are the lower vibrational base attitudes and emotions that separate man/woman from GOD.

GOD in Its most unlimited understanding is infinite love, joy, compassion and forgiveness; this is what needs to be taught. This includes a strong reverence for life, for the Creator is omnipresent in all Creation. There is no separation in omnipresence, and as Paul said, "When you are walking in love, you are walking with God; there are no divisions in God."

The Creator is truly omnipresent within all Creation. We are all sons and daughters of the Most High. "As pear seeds produce pears and nut seeds produce nut trees, God seeds produce Gods." (Meister Eckhart)

Ten Years of Base Poverty

I could not overcome my aversion to tithing and attaching money to spirituality. I believed money and Spirit must remain separate. Although people were coming and taking up my time and energy, there were few or no donations. Many made comments on how wonderful I was to devote my life and entire assets to serving in the awakening and healing of humanity and the Earth. They would drive up in their Cadillac, BMW or $30,000 auto, dressed in all the latest fashions. They would often be going through a spiritual or healing crisis, be in a traumatic relationship, or have lost a loved one, and would often receive clarity and healing from me. They would say thanks, express that a wonderful healing occurred, and leave.

When we would remind them that we could really use a donation to help keep the lights on, they would drop five or ten dollars in the basket and say, "Things are really tight this month." That night they would spend $50 to $100 on a restaurant meal, drinks and a show.

I would spend hours counseling people who said they were broke, healing their major past-life and childhood traumas, only to run into them the next day in a gift store, buying very expensive jewelry or a dress. A few months later, they would be back at the center, whining the same song: "I need help, I don't have any money," etc., etc. I believed that if I just kept the healing work as my first priority, the money would come and people would value the gifts.

After the NDE, I had the ability to read one's book of life. I could assist them in healing any past-life, birth or childhood experiences, quickly and gracefully. Upon removing these blocks and patterns, a rush of spiritual energies would flow in, and then people would receive conscious contact with their main teacher and guide.

There were many miracle healings occurring; I never knew when they were going to happen. I would tell them their healing was between them and Spirit, and that I can only try to get out of the way as best as possible, suggesting they do the same and let Spirit be their guide and healer.

One particular healing happened one day when a woman with severe back injuries came. Halfway through the counseling, she began weeping, loudly asking forgiveness. She had accessed a past life where she actually walked with Jesus and experienced the Crucifixion. She asked him to forgive her for not going to church in this life. He told her within, "Who do you think was inspiring you to not accept the graven images?" A great surge of energy went through her and she sat up erect. She was completely healed.

We asked her later, although she did reward us with a donation, to write a testimonial as to what had happened. She said, "No, I am a counselor and author. I cannot let people know I receive counseling from others."

Many other well-known authors, teachers and healers have come, as well as people in powerful positions in the fields of education and government; all have asked to remain anonymous. They're all afraid of being criticized or chastised for seeking alternative healing, which is not accepted within the mainstream. I found it sad that though powerful healings and awakenings were taking place, we could not get public support or even private support for the needs of the center.

Back to Basics

During those ten years, I learned many lessons. I went to work temporarily for the Forest Service; it was a contract job doing field surveys. I was a little too vocal about the condition of the forest and how, rather than preserving it, they were acting more like the Deforest Service. I walked by a room where they were going to show a film on forest management, and one of the staff asked me to join them. I said, "No thanks. I have already seen what you have managed to do to the forest. Better to just leave it alone. It can manage without us." What I did not know is that the head muck-a-mucks were in the room. Not surprisingly, they did not ask me back the next year.

I also worked doing odd jobs here and there—anything to supplement the center. I had to turn people away who wanted healing, especially those who had no problem watching me take a downward spiral economically. They loved to take up my time and energy, but when it came to a fair exchange of energy so that I could meet my own basic needs, they turned a blind eye.

Some even righteously made comments about how spiritual gifts are free and should be given freely. I told them, "While I was working with you, I could not be working elsewhere, and be sure and tell the phone and electric company, as well as the mortgage company, how spiritual I am and that they should ignore my debts."

I have learned that there is a fundamental flaw in the material society in which we live, where spirituality is put last on the list in terms of financial compensation. I have also learned there is an overall lapse in integrity within both the spiritual and business community when it comes to financial endeavors.

At night, sometimes into the wee hours of the morning, I worked on the first book. I received lots of information, but did not want to let it out until I was sure it was accurate. Many of the events prophesied were unfolding. However, I was struggling with sticking my neck out again, knowing that if one of the prophecies did not hit, I would never hear the end of it. Even if twenty were accurate and one missed, everyone would focus on the one miss. I knew that there would be those people like the ones before, living in a world of spiritual ego, full of attachment and denial, who would attack the messenger.

I was also struggling with the fact that the whole time, I could not get this question out of my head: "Where are they, the others who are truly dedicated to the awakening and healing process?" But something inside me continued to drive me forward. Although it made no common or economic sense to continue, I had to take the leap of faith and continue, knowing that as before, some way, Spirit would open a door. Several times I was a heartbeat away from losing the property, and just at the last minute, some miracle would happen to keep me hanging on a bit longer.

During this process I was having a vision of a woman coming into my life from the snow country. She had two children from a previous marriage, and when we met, there was an instant attraction. She was turning her life around, which had been filled with drug and alcohol problems, and she was living with her sister.

One night while having dinner at her house I saw her sister's boyfriend get really angry. There was an alcohol and drug problem there as well. It was getting really violent, and for the sake of the children I decided to have her move up to the ranch. It was very premature, for we had just met, but as a counselor I knew what happens to children when exposed to that type of environment. She agreed and before long, I had inherited a family.

Things worked out well for a while and we became really close. I assumed she was still regularly taking the steps necessary for birth control. Then, before I knew it, there was bread in the oven and I was about to be a father. I embraced the role, taking responsibility for my duties as a parent. We set up appointments with a naturopathic doctor who was also licensed in Western medicine; a payment schedule was worked out, along with birthing classes, and off we went. I prayed to Mary for help, along with AAA, which is pronounced "Eye Ay Ah," often referred to as the feminine aspect of God. She was well known in spiritual circles to assist the birth of children and one's birth into new awareness.

I knew I was going to need all the help I could get. Against my wishes, my mate went down to the welfare office. They said, "According to the father's income, we can pay for the birth and offer assistance." But I had already made payment arrangements with the other doctor and told her, "I do not want assistance. There is always a catch." She demanded to go through the welfare department and standard hospital procedures. I had to acquiesce, although I had a really bad feeling about it. Whenever the government says, "We are here to help," it is often to bury you in debt or take away your freedom.

The Birth of Alura

Before Alura was born, I was receiving guidance that the relationship with her mother was not going to work. I was completely committed, yet deep inside I knew the guidance was correct.

I began to connect with Alura's soul. She actually named herself, and she told me this was her path. She knew we would not remain together and that her mother would fall back into her old ways. She told me I must experience this, because how can I help others unless I know their pain? This was upsetting to me, and when I went to a name book that has the purpose listed with each name, I read that Alura meant divine counselor. From that point on, I could see how the universe, although on the outside seems very dysfunctional, is actually very functional.

We had one false labor, and then it was time. We rushed down to the hospital, while I was praying, "Please Lord, not in the car." We made it to the hospital, and things settled down. The medical staff waited for a day, checking to see if there were any complications.

At one time they said her water had broken and they needed to induce labor. I meditated on it and received really clear guidance that this was not the case. They checked again and said, "We will wait a little longer." The heart monitor started showing abnormal beats and they felt that something was wrong again. I went within again and was told the heart is fine—get a new machine. They did and all was well; it was a flaw in the machine.

I went out to take a break, and before going, I told them the birth would begin at 1:00 that afternoon, it would be a textbook birth, and all would be well. I also told them it would be a girl. We had skipped the ultrasound to see what the sex was, because I already knew. The doctor began to break out the oxytocin to induce labor, when I walked back into the room. I told him "It is not 1:00 yet," and he sat there, needle in hand, watching the clock. At one o'clock there was a scream and the birth had begun.

The nurses by that time were watching the chain of events, and rumors were going around the hospital. The doctor and our naturopathic doctor were both present, because the naturopath was a friend who had promised to be there. They asked, "What do you think? By the way she is carrying, it will probably be a boy."

I smiled and said, "A thousand bucks says it is a girl; we already know each other."

By that time my mate wanted to kill me. It was a tense situation which we were trying to cover up or break with a wisecrack or two—typical men stuff to avoid feeling the deep concerns. The doctors both looked at each other and seriously thought about taking the bet.

Alura's head soon popped out, along with the rest of her body. I moved from my position of holding my mate's hand, assuring her I was still there, and ceremonially cut the cord. I looked up and the room was filled with light; it seemed to come from everywhere. The nurses and the doctors all had a tear in their eye. There was definitely an angelic presence in the room. I was filled with so much joy at having a daughter, I felt like I would burst.

I went home later that night after they were asleep and took care of the other two children, bringing them to the hospital the next morning to see their new sister, after preparing breakfast bright and early. The nurses were also in the room, and after having seen the chain of events unfold, asked, "Are you a prophet?"

I told them "No, I am just awake."

The Separation

It was not long after Alura was born that her mother decided to fall back into her old ways. The welfare department told her she could get $800 a month if she moved out on her own. It was like telling an addict, "We will sponsor your addiction." She moved out and began drinking again.

Not only did they sponsor a life of drugs, alcohol and multiple sex partners, but they also started a lawsuit against me in order to finance it. My back went out again and I was laid up and could not get out of bed for quite some time.

I called the courthouse and they said, "Get a lawyer." I called every lawyer in the book and they said they could not help me due to my lack of income; call legal assistance.

I called legal assistance and they asked, "Are you in jail?" I said no and they said, "We are so overbooked, if you are not in jail we cannot help you."

The case was transferred from the local district attorney's office to the state offices, and one hand did not know what the other was doing. They put their bank of attorneys to work, imputed a wage to me that was over four times my income, and then had a kangaroo court session. I was not informed as to the date of the hearing until two days after the fact.

What they were doing was legalized extortion, based on known fraudulent information. There was a blatant lack of honesty, integrity and discrimination, due to the fact that I was not given equal opportunity under the law.

I wrote letter after letter, telling them that their information was incorrect and that it is on record that I qualified for assistance due to lack of income; therefore it was impossible for me to have the wages they were imputing. They ignored every letter and responded with liens and letters to everyone, demanding that people withhold any wages due me.

They sent letters to people I never worked for, my family, etc. They even demanded all payments from the publisher for my book. What they did not realize is that my publisher had only sent me a total of $50 for a book that went national; this was all recorded and given to them in my records.

On complete hearsay, without one shred of evidence, they decided I had separate accounts, hidden money and income; therefore they would not release the lien. They had set themselves up as judge and jury with no evidence.

When they found no income, they decided to put a lien on the property again, based on known fraudulent data. Finally I took them to superior court, where the true income was established and accepted, proving the state incorrect. When I took the court's decision back to them, they basically said, "We don't care," and continued the lien on the property, and then sued us for the entire amount.

I watched in disbelief how our own government now has arrogantly put themselves above the people and the courts. According to the courts, I owed a maximum of $14,000; I had paid over $18,000 on the lien, so I was $4,000 overpaid. They still demanded another $14,000 and refused to remove the lien. When asked, "Why won't you acknowledge the court's decision?" they arrogantly said, "Sue us." This is our government at work, serving the people. It was more like the Mafia, only this form of extortion was legal.

I took it all the way up to the State of Washington attorney general and the governor's office, praying there would be one official at the top that was not corrupt or too busy with their political career to help. They were now willingly and knowingly engaging in criminal activity. They all turned a blind eye and sent it back down to the very people committing what can only be termed as, I repeat, legalized extortion based on known fraudulent information.

I was finally granted a hearing with a supposedly unbiased board concerning my case. The board consisted of their attorney who was suing me, another welfare agent that was handling the case and a man who was also working for the welfare department. It was the most stacked, biased board I have ever seen. They could not answer my questions or come up with any proof whatsoever for their case. It was all hearsay and fictitious charges, yet they ruled against me.

This was another rude awakening concerning the corruption and blatant arrogance of our government. It is completely out of touch with honesty and integrity, and it has become an unjust disservice to the people. Politicians seem to be more concerned with their own careers and the sponsorship of big business than with serving the very people to whom they swore an oath. Truth, honesty, integrity and service are now foreign words in today's government. Despite our best efforts, the fraudulent lien is still in place and we have been continually harassed for over 16 years.

Forgiveness and Onward

Despite the outer appearances, I know truth will surface eventually. I have forgiven Alura's mother, the state attorney general, the governor, and the welfare department, which, given its course of action, could best be described as the warfare department. To this day I do not see how it serves a family to bribe the mother with funds on the condition that the family be split up, then financing a life of drugs, alcohol and multiple sex partners. As a counselor, this seems to be the height of incompetence.

Nonetheless, I continued to be the best father I could, given the circumstances, and never missed a birthday or Christmas, making sure Alura knew her father loved her. My sister continued to provide day care for Alura, and there I would spend time with her.

I knew that this was her chosen path, but it did not make things any easier. I know I will be able to help her much more later as she moves into her spiritual role, matching her name as a divine counselor.

In spite of all my domestic problems, a reforestation group and I were very active in saving the local surrounding forest. I could see both sides and was for preservation by stopping clear cuts, but was not against responsible logging.

One of the things my mate did was to want to invite the logging community to dinner and a few beers. This brought up some fear and anxiety in me, so I went out into the forest and meditated on it. What was revealed to me was that she had been my wife in the Viking lifetime. She was murdered because she took the children to another camp to buy some pottery. I told her not to go because there was tension between camps but she went anyway. They were all murdered, which threw me into a rage that continued throughout the entire lifetime. I was so enraged I picked up my battle-ax and laid to waste the entire camp almost single-handedly.

I could see now that we were working out the same events, only this time I caught it beforehand. I put my foot down and said, "No alcohol, no loggers."

The very next week there was an incident where a nearby gathering of people were descended upon by loggers and severely beaten. I understand the need for lumber, being a carpenter. What I do not understand is the clear-cut methods and total destruction of an environment. Clear-cuts are an abomination to God's creation and the sacred circle of life.

A Publishing Nightmare

During these trying times, I was also having problems with my publisher. We had made an agreement that was not being fulfilled, and after two years the book I had written, *Becoming Gods* (which has now been republished as *A Reunion with Source)*, went international and I had only $50 in royalties to show for it.

I had to ask myself, "What is wrong with this picture?" They were friends of mine, and had even sponsored my Intuitional and Inner Sensitivity Training class. I wondered how money always took precedence over Spirit.

There was a falling-out, the book was tied up, dead in the water, and I had to do something. The distributor went bankrupt, and the income from all the books that were sold vanished with the bankruptcy. There was very little promotion, and I knew inside that I had to get the book back.

I was told that although they would keep 92% of the sales, the volume of sales would compensate me for the percentage of money paid to them. In other words, due to their supposed expertise and promotional abilities, I would make more money than by doing it myself. The book was already selling well in a spiral-bound edition.

Two years later and $50 richer for the experience, I decided it was time to take back the book. Giving the publisher 92% of the proceeds for no marketing or promotion work on their part was unjust; I found myself doing almost all the promotion, with no compensation.

After several confrontations I finally received the book and all copyrights back. We revised the cover and made a couple of small changes, fixing a few errors. We had a wonderful photo (taken by Mona Leigh McCrea in 1996) of Mary's energy appearing over her statue next to Buddha's at the center, and we decided to put it on the cover. It seemed appropriate because her energies often came, together with Cazekiel's. A spiritual partner named Carolyn decided to create her own publishing company, and the new revised book was the first endeavor. Without her invaluable help, the books and the center may very well have fallen into extinction.

Mary's energy appearing at Sattva Sanctuary

Spaghetti with the Masters

One evening after meditation I decided to make spaghetti. I was alone, and contemplating all the adversarial experiences I was having. I knew my path would not be easy, yet I also was feeling very beaten up by the experiences. To me, life was supposed to be simple: love yourself and others, and live a life of honesty and integrity in service to the Source. How could one have so many problems?

I was looking at the karmic creations being worked out and the fact that one of the yogis had warned me that as I reached the higher planes of nirvana, the darkness would rear its ugly head. I knew I would be working out my karma in double time and the lessons would be hard, yet I also knew I would be the wiser and stronger for it.

While making the spaghetti, all these wonderful realizations were coming to me. I looked out the window, watching the snow softly falling, ever so thankful I had a warm meal and a fire raging in the livingroom woodstove. I pulled a little table and chair up next to the fire and began enjoying my dinner.

About halfway through the meal I began to see a pillar of light forming in the center of the living room. I looked out each window and up to the skylight, but there was no incoming light; there was a dense cloud cover and it was snowing. The pillar continued to form.

It reminded me of one of my meditations, when I went to a dimension where the first polarities started. The light and the dark intermingled with each other, swirling in a dance of positive-negative. The dark became the light and the light became the dark. However, this was more of a swirling column of light manifesting right in my living room. I projected my feelings into the column to sense its nature, and felt a divine feminine presence.

I had been working hard all day, and was exhausted. My knee and back were hurting, and I was supposed to go into town the next morning to do some clearing and healing work for a small spiritual group we had started in Hood River. I was indecisive as to whether I was up to it or not.

The column began to move towards me, and I said to myself, "Now this is going to be really interesting. I hope this thing is benevolent and that I am ready for this."

The column of spiritual energies stopped as if it felt my concerns. When I decided I was ready, it again moved towards me. As it got closer, I felt a cool grace and a quickening

Beam of light appearing over Sattva Sanctuary

energy; it touched my right knee and I began to tingle. A wonderful sensation began to move through my entire body, and in an instant my back and knee felt great and I felt rejuvenated. It moved back to its original position in the center of the room and began to fade.

What was funny was all I could say was, "Now that was interesting," with a big grin on my face. I found myself exceedingly happy. Shortly afterward I went to bed, deciding I had better get some sleep and go into town tomorrow for the gathering. The next day a friend of mine, who was a pilot, attended the meeting; it was a major healing and breakthrough for him. His main teacher and guide was AAA, often known as the Holy Spirit and feminine aspect of God. She was the column of white light that had appeared in my living room.

Other Gatherings and Glitches

I was asked by a women's group in Hood River to come and teach the Inner Sensitivity and Intuitional Training classes. It was a very advanced group that had already been deeply involved in metaphysics. I was honored and told them I would share what I know. I shared the lessons learned in the Tibetan Foundation, the Teaching of the Inner Christ and the eight years of yoga training with various yogis.

I had also learned various forms of process-oriented therapies designed to heal wounds, traumas and wrong conclusions from past experiences. This included techniques for healing childhood trauma and past-life influences as well. It was a wonderful class, and everyone shared in an open forum.

Before each class I would inform those attending, "I am not your guru, you are. If you follow me, you are lost, because you each have your own unique purpose. We are here to share some tools and techniques and understandings to help you know yourself, your true self."

The class was very empowering, and more like a gathering of masters than the usual student-teacher relationship. We taught techniques for healing unseen negative influences and discarnate spirits, etc., safeguards for pure inner guidance and advanced meditation techniques. We also covered the different planes and dimensions along the vibrational continuum. It was like a who's who in the universe.

I had asked the T.I.C. founder if she wanted to be a part of my center earlier, yet she and her staff declined when I told them it must remain open to all belief systems. They wanted to insure that their teachings remained pure. I understood their needs, but I had a different purpose, which was to bring all the teachings together. I was granted permission to buy their books, however, and use them at the center. Their book *Being a Christ* is a wonderful blend of East and West, minus the dogma, with powerful tools and techniques. I added it to the other tools, techniques and understandings from other teachings I had experienced.

One day as we were starting up a new class, one of their ministers appeared at the gathering, along with a friend who was also very involved with the ministry. We discussed the class and what would be involved, and at the end the minister stood up and said, "I am the only one qualified to teach this class. I was given this area as my domain. James is not a T.I.C. minister."

In this she was right. Although I had been involved in many institutions, I refused to become a minister of any one faith; I felt it separated me from the other faiths. I had taken the same training she had taken, except for the ministry part because of the aforementioned reasons. The main point was that mine was not a T.I.C. class; it was a sharing of many teachings.

It really put me on the spot. Do we war over God and divide the Earth into little mini kingdoms of God, with power struggles over territories and positions? This did not appeal to me at all. I stood up and addressed the class. I told them this was between them and Spirit. It was their class and if they would rather have her as a teacher, then I would honor their decision. All I asked was one thing: become a leader of self, not a follower. I then left the room.

I got into my truck, drove home, and went up to my little hill for guidance. I was very upset at the time, because I loved the people and the class and knew I was supposed to be there. I also knew I could not war over spiritual matters or fall into spiritual ego and competition. I did my usual clearing work, and a wonderful peace came over me. I heard within, "You did the right thing. All will be well; they have chosen."

I later received a phone call pertaining to what happened after I left. Several of the women stood up and made their points known. One said, "I am offended that you come in here presuming we need you, and you are to be our teacher. Look around you. There are two Science of Mind ministers, an author, a chiropractor and several nurses who have been in metaphysics for a long time. These are intelligent, powerful people. If you want to join us, you are welcome, but we asked James to come here and share with us. Incredible things have happened since." The others joined in with their comments. I could feel a warm glow in my heart as it began to open.

The phone rang again and again with the same message. I had mixed feelings, however. I was very honored, and at the same time felt sad that the other minister had chosen to engage in such a power play. I talked with her later and invited her to join us. There was always a little rift there, yet lessons for all.

The minister's friend whom she had brought with her came as well, and we became the best of friends and partners in the classes. We taught many classes together after that and she eventually moved up to the ranch. Her name was Laura Lee and she is a walking master of the highest wisdom.

Off to See Baba Ji

One night while in deep meditation, I found myself lifted out of my body in Santa Cruz and into the presence of

Baba Ji. We were deep in a cave underneath the Himalayas, and there were many people living there who were of a very advanced spiritual nature. I was sitting at the side of Baba Ji and he was talking to the others, praising me for talents I felt I did not have. It was very embarrassing.

I was praying that no one would ask me to do something spiritual or manifest something, because I was lacking in self-confidence at the time, especially when comparing myself to the abilities of Baba Ji. Baba Ji turned to me and opened his hand. There I saw several stones and crystals; one was a large piece of shiny gold. He wanted me to choose one. I looked at his hand and thought, "I know he wants me to choose the clear crystal for purity and clarity, but if I pick it I will never know about the others." So I went for the piece of gold. He quickly shut his hand, mixed up the stones again and opened his hand for me to choose again. I picked the clear crystal and he smiled.

There was a beautiful woman there who walked up to Baba Ji, dressed in a beautiful orange sari. She said she was going to go sacrifice herself. Baba Ji smiled and nodded and she started up a winding path to the top of a peak. The trail ended with a long drop into a shallow pool of water. I said, "Wait!" and begged Baba Ji to stop the sacrifice. He smiled at me and said, "It is ceremonial; no one dies." I felt extremely mortified, because she was sacrificing not her life but her lower nature on the peak—tossing it symbolically off the cliff into the pool down below. I was relieved and embarrassed at the same time.

I was then shown the grounds of the temple of Baba Ji. It was quite beautiful, with natural caves, waterfalls, gardens, and devotees and other masters blissfully going about their daily chores and rituals. I was told the woman was Mata Ji, often referred to as Baba Ji's feminine counterpart or paternal cousin. The temple is a beacon of love, joy, and spiritual wisdom for all to tap into.

When one makes a practice of connecting to Baba Ji through prayer and meditation, they themselves become a transmitter of the same spiritual energies. I snapped back into waking consciousness afterwards, wondering what that was all about. An overactive imagination? A dream? No, it was a real out-of-body experience, and the impact has stayed with me to this day. I found out later in a book that Baba Ji does still maintain a physical body and has an ashram that is described as being strikingly similar to the one in my experience. It is high in the Himalayas and is called Gauri Shankar Peetam.

Tent Meeting with Baba Ji

On a warm sunny day in the foothills of Santa Cruz, I was sitting in a tent, meditating with a yogi and several very powerful people, all very advanced on the spiritual path. A golden light descended upon me; my mouth began to twitch and my lips started moving all by themselves. It was one of the most bizarre feelings I've ever had.

The yogi turned to me and said, "Baba Ji wants you to speak." I was self-conscious (not the true self but the little self) and I declined. But Baba Ji was not letting me off that easily. My lips really began to have a life of their own. The yogi again said, "It is not proper to deny us the words of Baba Ji."

I told him, "I will do my best to speak what comes to me, but will not be responsible for screwing up the message." A wonderful message about the golden age of GOD came through. Baba Ji told us he would create the same energy in the tent to let us all experience the coming golden age. The energy was awesome. We felt no fear, no need. The security and bliss were wonderful, and all cravings and survival issues were gone. The usual "How will I pay the bills, what will I eat, how will I continue to obtain shelter?" and all the usual underlying survival thoughts and emotions, were gone. Not even the desire to seek love existed, because we were love. The funny thing was that all the cats in the neighborhood were climbing on the tent trying to get in. I guess they wanted to partake of the marvelous energies too.

After this, Baba Ji continued to guide me from within. His complete upper torso appeared one day over a pond where I was meditating. He has offered wonderful guidance and protection on my spiritual path, and there are no words to describe the admiration and appreciation I have for Baba Ji. He has been an ongoing part of my life and has manifested to many of my friends (some call them students) on a regular basis, guiding and clearing them of unseen negative influences. At the center, his upper torso manifested above the pond in an enormous figure, blessing the water and all who could feel his presence.

The Medicine Wheel

One of my most profound lessons came during a medicine wheel ceremony. There was a woman conducting it named Gladys. I always referred to her as the mother everyone wished they had, because she was extremely loving and cared deeply for everyone, yet it was tempered with the wisdom of us taking responsibility. She would hug you, listen to your story with compassion, and when all was said and done, she would make you take responsibility for creating the mess, helping you gain the wisdom from the experience.

The medicine wheels were very powerful and enlightening, and they helped people understand their connection to each other, the Earth, and the nature of both connections. There was an animal for each month of the year, a stone, an herb, plant or tree, and each person would learn about their nature and the nature of others when they would sit at the place designated by their birth. She would honor the four directions, Father Sky, Mother Earth, Grandfather Sun and Grandmother Moon, as well as the animal spirits of each direction. At the end we would meditate and focus on our totem animal or animal spirit guide.

While I was in meditation, an orca appeared, coming out of the mist. The wisdom emanating from the orca was overwhelming. At the end of the meditation I looked up and clairvoyantly saw Jesus above Gladys, arms outstretched, blessing the ceremony. This took me a bit by surprise. If anything, I expected a Native American elder or man dressed in buffalo robes, skins or a feathered headdress. I was told to tell her what I saw.

I went up to her and put my hand on her shoulder, telling her about the vision, and she began to weep and weep. I asked her if she was all right.

She told me her dad was a Baptist minister, and she had always been struggling with whether it was all right to do the medicine wheel. She knew in her heart that children need to make their Earth connection and start loving the Earth, honoring the sacred circle of life.

I told her, "I am sure Jesus approves, especially when it comes to the children." I also learned from this. I was told from within during the vision that a call to Spirit is always heard, no matter in what tongue it is made.

It is time to allow each individual their own path; let the many voices, each in their own way, sing as one harmonious chorus to the one Creator of all life. Separating into structured truths and arguing over names, images and doctrines are the follies of man. In heaven the Masters from all cultures walk arm in arm, for they have transcended all cultural and religious boundaries into a universal peace and love for all people and all life.

Encountering Nature Spirits

There were a lot of phenomena occurring at the ranch concerning nature spirits. Although I had heard many stories concerning their existence, I mostly just chalked them up to overactive imaginations or possibly something that occurred in some far-off distant past.

One day I was standing on a large boulder over the river, when it suddenly gave way. It split completely in half, sending me off the edge to land on my tailbone. It was a hard landing, right on top of the other half of the boulder that landed beneath my feet. I brushed myself off and limped back up to where the boulder split in two. I examined it very carefully to see if there were watermarks or a crack that had been there before I stood upon it. There was nothing. It was a large round lava rock and it looked as if it had been split by some unknown force. The rock was not weathered and had no watermarks that would show an already existing crack. I felt a presence that had something to do with the event.

I asked my guide Txosamarra what happened. He told me it was an angry gnome, very upset with the previous owner, who was unconscious concerning the land. The previous owner was a logger, and he left trash all over the ranch. He logged many of the old-growth trees, yet left a few along the creek areas that could not be farmed.

He also tried his hand at farming and used some chemical fertilizers, which was evident from the rusty barrels lying around. Luckily, the land had remained dormant for years before I bought it, allowing these chemicals to decompose; yet the gnome was still angry.

I asked Txosamarra to set up a meeting with the gnome. "Tell him my intentions for the land, and invite the gnome to work with us." This was done, and the gnome was elated to find out that I had a deep respect for nature.

I had acquired over 7,000 trees over the years, and was planting them to replace the forests. There was a lot of space that was not being used for farming, in which a variety of trees were introduced.

While on the outskirts of the property during my tree planting, I heard a voice. It said in a shy female voice, "I love you." I felt love permeated my heart, yet could not identify the source. I looked everywhere for a source of the words and the presence I was feeling, but there was nothing. There were no houses in the area, trails or people anywhere. This strange, mysterious, shy angelic voice came from nowhere.

I decided to meditate and see if I could find the source, and Txosamarra came to me from within. He told me it was a tree fairy. They are very shy, yet she wanted to express her gratitude for replanting the forest.

While out in my garden, I would see the plant spirits. I saw corn spirits that were very small; we had very small corn that year. I saw them again the next year and they were much larger. That year our corn grew very tall. I began to understand how each plant had its own spirit. I experienced gnomes, fairies and other Devas that worked with the nature kingdom, keeping everything in order, helping things grow. I found out I could work with them, and together we could create phenomenal plant growth and crop yields and have fun doing it.

Overhead fairy appearing at Sattva Sanctuary

Some of them are little tricksters; I myself have been accused at times of being rather impish. There are whole civilizations living right alongside of humanity, but most of humanity has lost the ability to communicate with other realms. There is a saying, "I will believe it when I see it."

In a world where consciousness creates reality, we choose what we want to experience. You have to believe it in order to see it, and have the reference points, or at least be open to the experience.

All I know is that my garden does not lie. The phenomenal growth and abundance, free of pests, stands as a testimony to what happens when one opens to the possibility of nature intelligences and chooses to work in harmony with them.

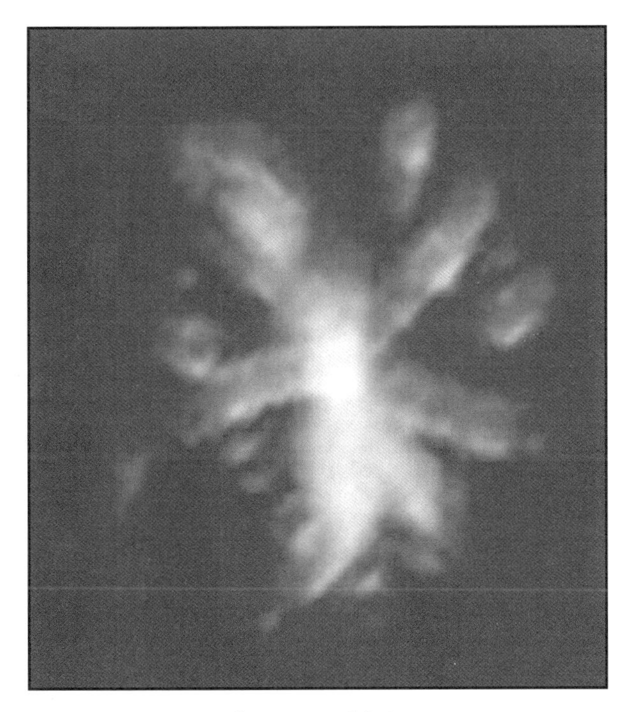

Blowup of fairy

Elves, Fairies, Gnomes and Star Nations Incarnate

Having experienced the energies of the elves, fairies and gnomes, I began to see many of these characteristics in humans. I soon realized that many humans on the Earth were more from these other realms than from our 3-D reality. They often have a deep respect for nature, are extremely sensitive, and you will most likely see them spending much of their time in nature. There is usually a sparkle in their eye, with a childlike innocence, and many have the same impish characteristics found in those other realms.

They often incarnate to bring the message from their world to ours that we need to start taking care of the environment. Being here in this vibration is very challenging for them, and some do not fare well.

There is a part of me that wants to gather them all up and create a community that lives in harmony with each other and nature, yet that would interfere with their mission to live where the need for their services is greatest. Of course, there is nothing wrong with coming up to the center and recharging once in a while.

Many of the children I have seen have the qualities mentioned above. They, along with souls from advanced Star Nations, are incarnating today more than ever before, as part of the awakening and healing process. I have seen many of these children. Some call them the Indigo Children, the super psychics of China, the Golden Children, etc. All of these children are very gifted and need to be honored and supported in their decision to come here. Their parents especially have a deep responsibility to assist them in maintaining these gifts or sacred senses. I have seen children with golden auras, some with every color of the rainbow and some with just one color, focusing on one particular gift.

Each ray of light has a particular consciousness that comes with it. Gold is the height of spiritual awareness, purple is also very advanced, blue represents love and wisdom, and green represents healing. These are just a few of the colors; there are many more, and mixtures of colors and consciousness.

The most profound experience I had with a child was with a very small, young girl. She was a package of pure bliss, her eyes sparkled and her smile beamed out pure ecstasy. When I walked by, she raised her hand towards me, reaching out and pulling her other hand out of her mother's. She came running to me, and I knelt down to greet her. The mother did not know what to do; her child had broken free and run to a perfect stranger. I looked up at her mother with a tear in my eye, grinning ear-to-ear, and told her, "Do you know who this is?"

Her mother, still feeling a bit defensive, said, "Yes, I think I do."

I told her to listen to her daughter. "When she speaks of things unseen, do not tell her they are not real. She is a gift to this planet."

I could tell that whoever came in contact with that child would not be the same. She was an example of pure innocence, and the power of love and joy that emanated from her was like nothing I had ever experienced. I saw the same sparkle in her eye that I had seen before in the fairy kingdom. Was she a fairy incarnate, an angel, an advanced soul from a far-off Star Nation? All I know is that the love, joy, and bliss that came with that little package is much needed on Earth.

White Eagle

At our retreat center, also called the Sattva Sanctuary, we hosted many different elders from different Indian nations. I was holding sweat lodge ceremonies on the full moon of each month, and one time a Cherokee elder said to me, "You have everything you need to do the sweat yourself." I did not want to offend anyone, however, and struggled with the idea. I knew the ceremonies and did not doubt my own connection to Spirit, but it was a big responsibility to run the sweat. My great-grandmother had walked the Trail of Tears, so genetically I felt I had it within my blood. I meditated all day and kept getting the green light.

The first lodge went very well. There was lots of healing energy, which seemed to make us feel higher than a kite, and the UFO's liked it as well. After sweat lodge they would often buzz us in approval. At some of the lodges there would be little lights dancing all about the lodge. Another time we heard wings flapping, which is a good sign. There was one lodge where a man in grief over his fiancée dying in an accident could not let her go. She appeared in the lodge, showing she was fine, and telling him it was time for him to move on. It was a great healing for him.

The most profound lodge for me was one time when it was filled to capacity, with over 25 people jammed in. During the singing and chanting, my arms slowly lifted up, as if they had a life of their own. A very powerful presence descended upon me, and we merged as one. My arms continued to rise, and extended out to embrace everybody in the lodge. They became like great wings folding around everyone. There were huge sighs and feelings of loving embrace felt by all. The energy held, and we became silent. Then my arms slowly returned to my sides, and the presence left. It was an encounter with White Eagle in which we were all extremely blessed.

Etheric Healing

One day I received a phone call from a very dear friend who told me about etheric healing. I was feeling strong energies pulsing through my hands, and they heated up during meditations. Then I came across a man from Africa (now residing in Belgium) who was well known for his healing abilities. When I saw his picture I knew instantly that he was a brother and that we had past-life connections. I could also feel he was connected to the same spiritual energies I was working with. He had a beaming smile of enlightenment that was contagious. His name was Eric, and he is president of the World Healing Federation. He was in Portland at the time, and I was invited to come to a healing session with a small group of people; I accepted.

When we met, it was instant recognition. There was a camera crew there doing a documentary, and he asked me if I wanted to have an etheric healing session. I agreed, and the next thing I knew, I was on the massage table. Eric held certain positions, with his hands just above my body; I could feel the energies moving through me.

While he was doing the session, I had called in my own healing guides and masters; I always do this as a precaution before meditating or receiving healing from others. I ask them to watch over the session to make sure that only spirits of the highest vibration come, and to protect me from any unseen negative influences.

Then something strange happened. While I was in an altered state with my eyes closed, he had moved towards my feet; yet I felt two distinct hands on my forehead. When I looked up, no one was there. It was as if his spirit continued to work on my forehead while he physically moved down the rest of my body. I had heard of his many successes in healing others, and I must say I was impressed after my own experience as well.

During the session, I kept hearing the photographers getting upset because none of their equipment would work. We were indoors and the flash would not operate; there were several cameras, and each refused to work. This had happened before, and I knew what the problem was: There was already too much light in the room. It was spiritual light, and the cameras were sensing it, yet the human eye was not sensitive enough to pick it up. Streetlights often do this; when I walk under them, they turn off because they think it is daylight. I always had fun after a yoga class; walking under streetlights and watching them go off one by one. One actually blew up from an electrical short. I was also guilty of blowing up other electronics from time to time.

I told the photographers what was happening and they refused to believe it. The combined energies of Eric and myself were shutting off the flash units. The photographers would go outside and the cameras would work. Upon returning to the room, the flash shut off immediately. Eric later came, on my invitation, and put on a wonderful workshop at the ranch, initiating me and a small group into the practice of etheric healing.

A few months later a good friend of mine went to India to learn some advanced yoga techniques. I told her I did not know why she kept looking outside of herself, because she was an extremely advanced being who had not yet owned her power. Her teacher in India forced a posture on her and she sustained nerve damage to her neck, which resulted in paralysis on one side of her face. She asked if I could help. I told her that it was up to her and GOD.

Eric taught us that you must become like a baby when doing the work. In the Native American ways, there is a saying that you must become like a hollow bone; allow Spirit to fill you. True healers get out of the way and allow Spirit to accomplish their purposes. They do not take responsibility one way or the other for the outcome. Sometimes there are karmic implications that will not allow the healing to occur, or there are lessons to be learned.

I knew my friend's main spiritual teacher and guide and invoked his presence, putting my hands on both sides of her face. My right hand began to heat up, and she was also feeling intense heat. She said it felt like her face was on fire. She knew it was healing energy and stayed with it, surrendering to the experience. The universe smiled upon her that day and the paralysis received a healing. I was told by her guide to tell her to stop seeking outside herself. She had all she needed to fulfill her purpose, and it was time for her to own her gifts and her divinity.

Teleportation to Portland

After teaching many sensitivity and intuition classes in the surrounding area, I was guided to go to Portland. It was an hour and a half away, but I felt I had to go because the classes were diminishing in my local area, due to its small population. There was a yoga teacher in Portland that I had become involved with, and she wanted me to come and teach the classes. I agreed, and soon was driving into Portland once a week. In between classes, I was helping a friend remodel a house in The Dalles, Oregon.

One particular day my back was really aching. I asked for a healing as I was driving, some relief to make the journey a little easier. What happened next was unbelievable.

I remember spacing out for a second; I had just left The Dalles and was on the freeway for only a few minutes. The next thing I knew I was in Portland, on the freeway right where I was to get off to go to the house where I taught the classes. I did not remember anything in between.

There was no memory of scenery, nothing I was used to passing in my usual drive to Portland. I knew there was no way I could have passed out and made it all the way to Portland without hitting something. Next, I looked down at my clock; it read just ten past eight o'clock, and I had left The Dalles at eight o'clock, after having breakfast with my construction partner.

I walked into the yoga teacher's house and she was amazed, because I had just called her before I left. She said, "Real funny; you were already in Portland." I told her to call over at the house where my partner was and tell him that I was at her house, and I dialed the number for her. He answered and she said, "Was James with you this morning?"

He said, "Yes, we had breakfast; he is on the way to your house. He will probably be there in an hour and a half."

She told him I was there, but he could not believe it. I got on the phone and told him I was there. He still did not believe it, and thought we were playing a prank or something. Both of them consulted later. I did not find out what happened until afterward. It was my first experience in teleportation, car and all.

In Hot Water

When I returned from Portland, we were putting the finishing touches on the house in The Dalles, getting it ready for a renter. The vice-principal of the high school wanted to rent it, and needed it immediately. We were working as fast as we could to finish, and he showed up just when we were trying to light the water heater. I tried everything to light it but it would not, though it was brand new. I checked all the valves, made sure they were open, went back to the pilot light, and tried again.

The new tenant was getting upset, because he had a plane to catch and needed to take a shower. I put my hands on the water heater and prayed, "Please light; we need hot water." The prospective tenant made it very clear that if we did not have the house in operable condition, the deal was off.

He said, "I am going to take a shower anyway, even if it's cold." He jumped in and took...a steaming hot shower. When he came out he said thanks, and the steam was still pouring out of the bathroom. We said, "For what?" and he said, "The hot shower."

Darwin my partner said, "You could not have taken a hot shower; we never lit the water heater. Besides, it could not have heated up that fast."

We went into the bathroom and found the water was steaming hot, then went back to the water heater and there was no flame or pilot light. The gas company man came out a couple of days later and said there was a plug in the line. He removed it and showed us there was no way we could have gotten any gas, because it was plugged at the meter over three weeks ago.

My partner owned the local Mexican takeout restaurant and often talked about integrity and honesty, as well as how spiritually motivated he was. It was a partnership that unfortunately later became a dictatorship, with all the proceeds going into his pocket.

My half of the proceeds, once the house was sold, was to go to the center, and I went deep into debt while finishing the project. I was counting on the funds to cover some back payments on the ranch taxes, and other things. Even though I was going into debt, however, I kept my end of the bargain. My word has always been law, to be honored just as my father's was.

It is funny how when the money comes, we forget our commitments and rationalize away our integrity. He did not have any money to pay me, yet somehow he managed to buy a brand new BMW. Shortly after that, he had a new $40,000 Land Rover.

What was ironic was that he looked just like my brother's old partner, who had also betrayed a trust. It was like someone had stamped them out of the same mold. A psychic friend did a reading and said they were like cold ovens; the outside looks warm and inviting, but nothing is on inside. It was obvious that outer appearances and the material world took first priority, over my partner's soul and spirit.

I remember a saying by Confucius: "When a man says trust, trust, trust, it is time to count your spoons, spoons, spoons." Those funny word—betrayal and trust—kept coming up for me. I really wanted to trust people; I wanted to believe they were honest and had integrity, but I kept experiencing the betrayal part when it came to sharing the earned funds previously agreed upon.

The Golden Panel of Spirits

One day in deep meditation I found myself in front of a golden panel of beings. There was a large, curved, golden table that looked more like a long desk. I saw nothing else in the room, for it had no walls, just a white mist. It seemed to be a spiritual manifestation, rather than a physical place.

I was standing before what looked like a tribunal or conference, receiving instructions. Many of the beings I recognized; they were Masters from all faiths and cultures. Some were extremely spiritual off-world Masters that in physical appearance were definitely not what one would be accustomed to.

I was later told that they were the overseers behind the retreat center and my work on Earth and that I, like many others, was receiving instructions. I could not remember the instructions but was told not to worry; they are in my subconscious and would be there when I needed them. I realized I was not alone, above or below on Earth.

Many people are receiving information directly into their subconscious while sleeping or out-of-body, and this information will aid them in fulfilling their destinies in "the awakening and healing process." If they meditate frequently, it will be easier to have conscious awareness of the ongoing spiritual meetings on other levels. Most people are unaware of these meetings, because it is very hard to bring the memory through the veil into 3-D mental, emotional and physical awareness.

Building the Pyramid

In a dream one night, after a long meditation, I was shown a golden pyramid. After I saw the pyramid, a bolt of energy jolted me in the chest and knocked me a foot up into thc air. It came out of nowhere. It did not hurt, but it received my immediate attention—a subtle hint, so to speak, that it just might be a good idea to build a pyramid for a healing and meditation room.

I had a large 20x20 building with no roof, and I was going to put a second story up anyway. I meditated on it and got a strong pulse of energy that it would be best to build it there. However, I had no knowledge of how to construct a pyramid, and I continued to meditate on it. I was shown how to cut the proper angles and fasten the boards together.

I was like a possessed man, working from early morning until night, just like I was when building the Bridge House. There was an energy that seemed to be endless, inspiring me to finish. It was a new presence, yet was of the Christ vibration. I kept asking myself, "Where am I getting the knowledge to build this?"

Then the pulse of energy hit me again. The name Pythagoras came to me, along with another bolt of energy. Now it all made sense. Someone with a higher knowledge of geometry was acting like a divine cheerleader.

I started researching Pythagoras and the Pythagorean Society, and discovered that it was a very advanced society that taught spirituality, the arts, high math and sciences, and the members were vegetarians, for the most part. They were one of the first societies to treat women equally and teach them along with the men. Obviously there was a higher purpose unfolding on the land.

Ramtha Again

After the first meeting with Ramtha, I decided that without a doubt, he was for real. His teachings were impeccable. J.Z. Knight made a few mistakes (what she calls experiences) from which she gained wisdom in her life, and she readily admitted to them. It caused a lot of problems and rumors, but, as we all know, anyone on the forefront of new knowledge that challenges the status quo is going to be under fire.

It is my belief that we have to give these pioneers some slack, allow them to be human, and support them through their lessons. Before I teach classes, I begin by telling people I am not infallible, and that I have my own lessons. I was never a joiner or follower, so I usually learn things the hard way.

I liked the empowering message of the Ram, but the second meeting was a lot more than I bargained for. It was a very small group in the pool area. We were lined up in chairs, and Ramtha came out in the usual fashion and began addressing the group, starting with the other side of the room. I was listening to the questions in a somewhat altered state myself, the energy being very high. There were many questions being asked, and I was going within and coming up with the same answers. It was like tapping into a flow of consciousness, and I was really having fun with it, feeling rather smug at how well I was doing.

Ramtha then turned from the other side of the room, pointed right at me, and said, "Master, what say you?" There was a force focused upon me that seemed to go right through me; it really caught me off-guard. I wasn't ready for the sudden influx of energy or to engage in outer conversation; I had no questions and had come only for the experience. I simply wanted to enjoy the consciousness and energies present during the channeling.

I got a grip on myself and said, "I just came for the mirror."

Ramtha did not let me off so easily. He said, "What do you see?"

I said, "I see a very wise and powerful, loving being."

He said, "Master, what you see is you. If it were not within you, you could not see it. It is time you own it."

From that point on, I knew it was time to walk my talk and live the teachings in a more profound way. On the way out, I saw a table with some tapes. One in particular was titled "Inner Earth," and I felt an undeniable urge to buy it. When I went home to listen to it, lo and behold, everything and more of what I had witnessed with the Tibetan Foundation was on it. It was a real confirmation.

I later had an encounter with the same small entity from the Inner Earth. His message was the same: it was time for the surface dwellers to clean up their act, ASAP.

The June Affair

Despite the earlier angelic messages concerning my need to master interpersonal relationships, I swore off women for a while. I was very content with being alone. It was less complicated, and allowed me the freedom to devote my full attention to the center and spiritual growth.

I was teaching a class in Portland, and in walked June. She was the woman of every man's dreams—blonde and beautiful, with a body that would stop traffic. She also professed a high degree of spirituality, and was a therapist. It was like a dream come true—an instant attraction that transcended the physical.

I had one major reservation: she was very much into outer appearances. She drove a white Jaguar, had lots of gold, and her clothes and the cost of her makeup alone could have bought a much-needed tractor.

The package also came with two teenagers, the ultimate challenge. When you have two teenagers where the past form of male discipline was giving them $50 and saying, "Get lost so I can be with your mother," you're screwed from the start. Not even God can fix that one. But of course I was going to try. All I could do was to be an example, and try to be there for them when they asked. Whenever I tried to get them to help on the ranch, however, it was like pulling teeth. Any assertiveness on my part was responded to with "You're not our father," etc., etc.

I had hoped that being out on the land would open them to a different reality; they had been getting into a lot of trouble in the city. June and I spent much time together before making any big moves, yet the energy and connection between us was so intense that people said they could cut it with a knife. The attraction was undeniable and unstoppable. I decided that maybe it was time to give up my solitude for a while; after all, she would definitely be an asset to my life and to the center.

The first year together was incredible. There were a few glitches like with any young romance, then as the love began to build between us, so did the fears and unresolved issues.

Love and passion can be a double-edged sword. When a couple moves into greater depths of love, deep wounds can begin to surface. Your little love muffin becomes Atilla the Hun. Eventually, there is a lot more Huny than honey.

It seemed I could do nothing right, and there was nothing good about me in her eyes whatsoever. I even asked one day, "Is there anything you like about me; one thing you could compliment me on?"

There was a long pause. She said, "Yes."

I asked, "What?" Another long pause, and she was off on a new subject. This did not change my love for her, however, nor did I need her approval and acceptance. I was just working towards reestablishing a complementary union of mutual respect.

I had an ace in the hole concerning relationships. I have found that when one is dependent on the love, acceptance and approval of another, they are on an endless roller coaster ride, because people are fickle. Their love, acceptance and approval ratings usually fluctuate, especially when the women are processing and their issues are coming up. You become their father, and every other man that lied to, abused or betrayed them. With men, women become their mothers, and every other woman who lied to, abused or betrayed them as well.

Relationships are tough right now, because the whole world is going through a healing process. A master teacher told me that the only reason anyone has any power over you is because you want something from them. Be it love, acceptance or approval, all of these are to be found within self. Then you can love unconditionally without attachment, like the Sun sending you warm, loving rays, evenly and consistently. It is called the flow.

This was my initiation into the flow. It was as if the universe said, "We are going to test your steadfastness to the flow," and began to hit me with all it had.

They say, "What doesn't kill you will heal you." I think I walked that edge for the rest of the relationship. I had to finish the house in The Dalles, so I was spending long hours there. This began to bring up all her issues.

There was also a very wealthy trust funder who was chasing her and calling the center, acting as if he needed her to heal him. An ulterior motive was definitely at play here; I sensed it from the very beginning and brought it up to her. It was a recurring pattern, because part of her was insecure and yearned for an extravagant lifestyle. It wasn't the first time some wealthy entrepreneur kept calling the house and sending gifts.

She would assure me that they were just friends, yet a little voice inside me said, "Not so." Both of her wealthy men friends would show open displays of anger and jealousy concerning our relationship, which made the truth of the matter pretty obvious. While she was keeping these men on the line, she accused me of having affairs while in The Dalles. She even accused me of being bisexual and having wild parties with other men when I was remodeling the house.

June's previous marriages had all ended very tragically, with one betrayal after another. Her own brother was gay, and it seemed she had not completely dealt with that, or her hurt might have stemmed from her fears and wounds from a previous marriage. The previous relationships had some really bizarre activity going on, spanning the entire dramatic spectrum, which I will not delve further into here.

Meanwhile, all of this was being projected onto me. I sat her down and told her I loved her, and that I would not do such a thing as cheat on her, let alone sleep with men. I said, "It is completely against my nature, and there is neither the desire, nor even the curiosity about it. I am as honest and loyal as the day is long. You are going to have to trust one more time.

"Here is a key to the house I am remodeling. You are welcome anytime, as you always have been, to drop in. If you want to hire a detective, by all means do so. I have nothing to hide. All you are going to see is pictures of one dirty, hard-working construction worker."

When one can no longer project their issues and blame another, thus validating their fears, they will often find another person who will participate or act out these dramas, rather than go within and heal them. The pain is often too great to face within, so they will try to recreate the situation without, in the physical.

A few weeks later, she was doing the very thing she was accusing me of—having an affair. The rich trust funder was playing on her fears, telling her I was gay and also having sex with all the women in my Self Mastery class. However, most of the women in the class were married, and their husbands were in the class with them. I had also invited her to join the class and she did on several occasions. This was a classic example of accusing others of what you yourself are doing.

The desire for the extravagant lifestyle and the constant bribes offered to her by the wealthy trust funder, along with his playing on all her fears, finally won out. I was off to work one morning, and had to turn around and go back into town to pick up some supplies for the job. As Spirit usually puts me right in the right place at the right time, there I encountered June at a local restaurant, having breakfast with the trust funder. There was a thick gray cord of energy between them, attached to the first three chakras that represent survival, sex and power. It was obvious that his tactics had worked; the affair was happening and I was no longer in the picture. To remain in this relationship would be to live a lie.

I came home that evening and told her what I had seen. She continued to deny it, yet I was also told by others that she was having an affair. She confided in some friends who were also friends of mine, and they felt that, although it was a struggle for them, disclosing this information, they thought I should know. I thanked them, and told them I was aware of it. I told her I knew what was happening, and that we would no longer be sharing a bed. She now had a choice to make.

Then I came home the next day and put flowers all over

the entire bed, and told her I loved her. I had already forgiven her and knew I could not stop the flow of love, and had to keep my heart open. A 14-year-old girl had taught me that. She was very clear and was receiving visions (Isis was coming to her in dreams), and her mother asked me to work with her to help her understand what was happening. While I was showing her how to insure pure channeling and establish a few safeguards, Isis came in. She told me, "You have to keep loving, no matter how hard it hurts. Only love will free you."

I remembered those words and, despite what was happening with June, I knew I had to keep my heart open. I also had another little trick up my sleeve. I was in constant contact with the nurturing feminine energies of Mary. Mary the divine Mother was sending me love feedings that far surpassed any Earth love I had ever experienced.

There was one final blowup, and then the June relationship was over. Of course, I had to be made the demon in order to validate her choices; thus I was again accused of everything in the book, all of which had no basis in reality.

I knew there was nothing more I could do, and the center now had to take priority. She demanded that I move out, and I told her I had built the center for the purpose of anchoring in the light and assisting in the awakening and healing process. It was not to be a place for illicit affairs and the material-minded, "See me, dig me," crowd.

Under protest, she moved out shortly afterward. I was both sad and relieved at the same time. The energy at the center had become very scattered, and I asked one of the Masters if what had transpired had done any permanent damage energetically. He said, "Nothing that cannot be repaired and cleaned up."

Feathered Friends

Although I was saddened by the breakup, I was not devastated. There was a part of me that doubted myself, however, even though I knew I had acted honestly and honorably throughout the relationship. One time I had lost my cool, but regained it quickly. Still, I had to be self-analyzing concerning the recurring pattern. Was I a real chauvinistic womanizer in a past life who had tortured women, and this was my karma? Why was this recurring? I knew I had betrayal patterns, and that there are no victims. I was drawing women to me who were destined to betray me. I had healed many of them, yet there seemed to be something I missed.

I went into deep meditation and asked, "Please show me the lesson." I then saw myself as a king in a past life, with June as my queen. However, I always felt she was with me not for love, but for the power, position and wealth. The trust funder now represented the wealth and the power that money can buy, but he did not possess any true power—that comes from love, compassion and a life of service without ulterior motives. I saw that I was given a second opportunity to see how she really felt and what her true priorities and values were. When I died in that lifetime, this was my last thought: "Did she truly love ME?" It was all making sense.

The next morning, I went to work at another house I was doing some repairs on in Hood River. I was putting up some siding, hammer in hand, banging away. I was still self-analyzing and feeling doubt about whether I was right about the past or was just fooling myself. Maybe I was a real jerk. I stopped for a moment, turned around, and a bird flew up and landed on my shoulder. It just sat there, chirping away, and a feeling came over me. I thought within, "I can't be all that bad if birds are landing on me." It was an evening grosbeak, and they are usually very wary.

The woman that owned the house came out and saw the bird sitting on my shoulder. She said, "Is it hurt?"

I said, "No, it just flew up and landed on my shoulder." It was singing away fearlessly.

I picked it up on my finger and she said, "Did it hit the window or something?"

I said, "No, it is fine."

She said, "Wait, I want to get my camera, but it will probably fly away."

I said, "I do not think so; it seems to have a message or reason for being here." She went inside, got her camera, and took a few pictures. I have them to this day as a reminder. Whenever I am seriously challenged or slandered for bringing in the light, I just remember the bird and how I can't be that evil or the birds would not land on me. It happened other times as well, just to show me it was not a fluke.

James with a bird on his shoulder

Fully Devoted to My Center

I decided to put all my energies into the center again. Although I was told earlier that it was my purpose to learn about basic interpersonal relationships, I was now ready for the cave again.

A yogi told me that the path of relationships is the

hardest path to master. He was right. I have always gotten along well with animals, children and Masters. It is these adults, with all their preconceived ideas, beliefs, desires, wants, wounds and traumas, who were the most challenging. Couldn't I just build a center for children and animals? The problem is that children have this appendage called the parent, so you have to clear everything with the parent in order to reach the children. If you step out of the adult's belief system, the mother's instincts kick in, and you'd better take cover.

So how do we bring in these teachings which are in direct contradiction to the status quo? The fundamentalists hate you, because you are putting the temple back within the individual and taking away the tools of fear, guilt and unworthiness that they use to keep the masses under control.

The disenchanted Christians hate you, because they want nothing to do with anything that resembles another enslaving religion, even though we empower the individual to make their own personal connection to Source. The name Jesus gets their back hair up, because of all the false images taught to them as children.

The material-minded people care only about their next toy and outer appearances. The loggers want nothing to do with us because we want to preserve things, and the environmentalists feel we are in denial because we are not demonstrating and tying ourselves to trees.

Being out in the middle of nowhere also made it tough to generate some interest. Many a day I had to ask myself, "What is the point?" yet I knew deep inside that there was a higher purpose unfolding and we were to hold the frequency. It was a special place of the highest vibration, and the land needed to be preserved. People who were sensitive felt the energy as soon as they set foot on the land. There were many healings and awakenings happening on a regular basis at the center, but for some reason it just wasn't growing, and the income was next to zip. I kept asking Spirit and myself, "Where are the other visionaries?"

Shadow the Horse and Lessons on Death

A very good friend of mine named Don came up the driveway one day and asked me if I wanted another horse. I had an old Arabian already, named Kima. I usually let other people pasture their horses on the land to keep her company, but she seemed to be as reclusive as I was at times. He took me to see a very large black horse that was scheduled to be slaughtered. Shadow was part workhorse and part quarter horse, and I could tell she had a lot more life in her. I decided to buy her to insure that she was not made into French hamburger, which was where she was headed. I spent many wonderful hours riding that horse. We became very close friends. She was my kind of horse—incredibly surefooted, and she was like riding a tank. She was built like one too.

One day we were asked to pasture a large black stallion. Shadow and Kima had become good friends, and Shadow was like a protective mother. The stallion kept trying to get to Kima, but Shadow would step between them.

One day the stallion was rearing, pawing the sky, and decided to take Shadow on. He came running up to her at a full gallop. Shadow lunged at him as he reared, and the next thing I saw was the stallion flat on his back. Shadow one, stallion zero. That was the last challenge; they got along well after that incident.

Then Shadow became very ill. She had what the vets call twisted gut. Her eyes were very glassy, she went down and could not get back up, and her breathing was very shallow and labored. The vet and a good Native American friend said there was nothing we could do; better arrange for a backhoe to come in the morning, because she would be dead by then.

I stayed up all night with her. We fed her chamomile tea and garlic, and I lay next to her and prayed. The next morning she was up and standing, clear-eyed, drinking water and eating. The vet and my Native American friend came the next morning to check up on things and could not believe their eyes. She seemed very healthy, and for over a month she showed no signs of being sick.

Just before sundown one evening, I saw her looking to the west at the sun and nodding her head up and down. It was like a ceremony. She would bow down and just keep nodding. I knew I had to go out to see her, and she continued to bow and nod as if I was not there. She then walked over to me and bowed one time, very low, lifted her head up, and I instinctively said good-bye. Her spirit ascended above her physical body, and she dropped dead. I sat down by her side and cried.

After a while I looked up to the heavens and said, "One horse. I don't ask for much, just one horse. After all I have done in service, just one horse." That was all I asked for myself: to heal one horse. I sat back down and cried a little more.

Then a message came to me. I saw very clearly that I was interfering in her soul's evolution. It was her time, and had been her time when I had saved her from the butcher. I knew Shadow was getting old and could not keep up with the other horses; she could hardly run anymore. It was time for a new vehicle, for hers was old and worn; it no longer served her spirit.

Just then, my Native American friend came up and put his hand on my shoulder and said, "Do they have horses in heaven?" What was strange was that when humans die, I know where they are going, due to my own death experience. It affected me more to have my horse die. I guess it was time to offer them the same benefit of the doubt.

"Yes," I said, "they have horses in heaven." The following year, my other horse, Kima, was killed by a mountain lion. She was very old, and it was her time as well. She fought the cougar off, and did not die right away. I dressed her wounds and spent the evening with her, as I had done with Shadow. I prayed for the Masters to come and either heal her or take her away, and I burned sage all around her during my prayers. It was getting late and I fell asleep. I had a dream that she came to me and asked that I take her to the high country. I did, and when she left, she shape-shifted into a deer and ran off into the forest.

When I awoke, I knew she was gone. I saw her lifeless body, yet knew she was at peace, moving on to greater heights in her soul's evolution.

Bound for Tahoe and Another Relationship

A woman named Alice came to visit Carol, a late friend of mine. Carol was a character; we had a lot in common, and she sponsored some Inner Sensitivity and Intuitional Training classes at her home. She was one of the few people I could feel comfortable around, where we could be our outrageous selves.

Alice was introduced to some of the healing techniques we often used—one healing technique in particular, that usually results in a quantum leap in consciousness. She could also feel the energies of the Masters we worked with. In her own words, she said that in her vast spiritual journey, she had "finally found the gold." She invited me to come to Tahoe to lecture, and teach some Enlightenment Intensives.

It had been a while since I had been off the mountain; I was really enjoying my semi-reclusive, simple life. I meditated on it, and received a clear message that it was time to come down.

I was received very well in Tahoe. The lectures were packed, and I was doing counseling from sunup to sundown. I also made a lot of new friends. It was a different world, however, from that of the center. There were a lot of interpersonal relationship dramas, not just with couples, but with groups. Watching the dynamics, the love and power struggles, the praise and gossip all mixed into one that comes with any community, was interesting.

I was not without my own dramas while I was there. I

had visions of meeting a woman where there were some unresolved past-life issues and other work for us to do together. She would not know the extent of my work, and some things I could not share with her. It had a lot to do with healing personal relationships with men, as well as some other spiritual practices she was involved in. White Eagle showed me visions of the work I had to do. I could not complete all of it, but was told that I had done all I could do for the time being, and it was time to leave.

The second visit to Tahoe was very similar to the first—lectures and counseling, only this time I took a little time for myself to play. I met a woman named Jean, and the attraction was overwhelming. I have learned from the past that, whenever there is a really strong attraction, there is usually some past-life karma to finish.

Jean was married at the time, but I was informed she was separated. I found out later that the separation was not really that separate. According to her, the last five years were not good, and she and her husband were separate in every sense of the word. Although I had a strong connection and feeling for her, I did not act upon it; we remained just friends for quite some time. I told her I did not do triangles, or date married women. I also told her she had to work things out with her mate, and I did not want to be the reason for the breaking up of a marriage.

Try as I might to deny my feelings, the attraction would not leave. No matter how hard I tried, I could not walk away. I was even confronted by her husband, for whom I felt deep sympathy because of his pain. I told him very clearly that I had not acted on my feelings for his wife, and I told her she had to work things out at home. I also told him I could not control her feelings. No one can control another person's feelings, and no matter how hard we want someone to feel differently, the change is not up to us. All we can pray for is the highest and best good for all.

The husband's mother had run off with a minister and left his father very bitter; it had affected the son as well. I could see the dynamics unfolding, and how each person had an opportunity to heal. It did not make things any easier, however, for I could feel his pain, and I felt somewhat responsible. It was tearing at me from within. His pain, along with my own desire to be with her, was eating away inside of me. I stuffed my own feelings and walked away.

She tried to make the marriage work one more time, but it continued to go downhill. When I returned to Tahoe they were finally separated, yet there was still a lot of friction. My desire for her was still as strong as before. Never in my life had I felt such love and desire for any woman. When we embraced, it was the most passionate, heartfelt, expanded love I had ever experienced. She would tell me she loved me beyond all human understanding, and I felt it.

What was revealed to me was that we were together in a past life in the 1600s. We were about to be married, and the castle was being attacked. There were only a few of us inside, and we men became the first line of defense. We ran out without armor—just a sword, shield and sandals. We had to slow the attackers down so that the gatekeepers could shut the gates, but we were greatly outnumbered, and I fell at the hands of the enemy. My last vision was of my beloved watching from above. Now I knew why the desire was so overwhelming; it was an unfinished love, carried over for hundreds of years.

Our current love was a long-distance romance. I could not be with her all the time, since I had a center to finish and run, and she had a nursing career in Tahoe. We were making plans to live together, and the passionate, loving phone calls and letters continued.

My grandmother used to say that absence makes the heart grow fonder. Then she would add, "of someone else." In this case, she was right.

There was a doctor who also had designs on Jean. He bought her flowers, dined her, and took her on missions of mercy to far-off lands. He also promised her security and a good job at the hospital. You can guess where it went from there. She wrote me passionate letters all the while, yet intuitively I knew.

The last time we were together, I remember looking at her at the airport. There was a dark energy that seemed to come over her, and I knew at that moment that it was over. Nonetheless, I tried to work things out. I remembered the passionate love and joy we had had when together. I never could understand how one would not hold that to be precious above all else. To go from a passionate love beyond all human understanding to cruel, cold-heartedness, with no explanation in-between, is something I will never comprehend. It took me a long time to heal that relationship. To this day, there are a few unanswered questions.

Loving Detachment, the Hard Way

I was on the spiritual fast track, cleaning up my past-life experiences and learning one of the hardest, most challenging lessons: loving detachment. I knew, as Isis once said through the innocence and wisdom of a 14-year-old, that you have to keep loving. I could not afford to shut down my heart and expect to stay on the spiritual path. After all, God is a feeling: love. I had to find a way to continue to let love flow through me, despite the lack of love from others, and their sometimes cruel nature.

I remembered once when I asked the Masters in the unseen, "How do you view us, with all of our screw-ups, trials and tribulations?"

They said, "With loving detachment." They also said, "We have mastered judgment. Our love, joy and bliss are not determined by the thoughts, feelings or actions of another. We do not seek love, joy and bliss; we became them."

Another Master once said, "The only reason anyone has any power over you is because you want something from them. Be it love, joy, acceptance, approval or security, all these things are to be found within self."

I was being given a crash course in these very understandings. If the lessons did not kill me, I knew I would emerge all the stronger and wiser. I was becoming a master of mud, throwing myself into deep pits of relationship sludge, pulling myself up and washing myself off.

It is easy to maintain bliss while celibate in a cave, away from society. To do it in social consciousness, on the front lines, is another story. To do it in a passionate relationship is the greatest test of all. Maintaining your center, despite the whole of the world and its chaos, is quite a challenge.

I was always struggling within, vacillating between the desire to be ascetic and the desire for a mate. I had read where all the ancient gods of India and the patriarchs of old in every culture seemed to be married. Even Shiva was married, and it is well known by many scholars that Yeshua ben Joseph, the one called Jesus, also took a wife, had kids and continued to live out his life in India.

I could not understand how being embraced by the passionate arms of a woman, her warm breasts pressing against mine, with us energetically and spiritually merging in ascending spirals of love and bliss into the heavens, how this was wrong. Denying the physical embrace of a mate as something other than God, the Creator within all Creation, never made sense to me.

I was still trying to find balance between relationships and Spirit. It is an ancient tug of war. Almost every Master had their greatest awakenings in the wilderness. Nature does not judge you; it is the best reflector of God and your divinity. The master teachers around the world spent much of their time in nature, moving in and out of the cities. They would go out into nature to recharge and remember, because in the chaos and confusion of the cities and social consciousness, there are very few mirrors.

Very few people know how to just be. They are in constant seek mode, chasing the almighty dollar, love, sex, and acceptance and approval outside of self. Many believe that self-worth is established through outer appearances and positions of power. Some believe that their security depends on this as well. They also believe that their joy comes from others or from material objects. However, no one can make you feel anything; it is your choice each moment what you want to feel.

Material objects do not possess emotions. Emotions are generated and felt within. Those who believe they will be happy and that their self-worth depends on the new car and the outer appearances have, in error, attached these attitudes and emotions to a material object. One of the greatest traps is depending on others for one's love, joy, acceptance and approval. These games are the games of social consciousness. They are enslaving.

Fourteen Fundamentalist Ministers

Early one morning I awoke to a phone call from a local minister. He said there was a gathering of ministers from the area who wanted to come and talk with us. There were many rumors going around town that we were Satan worshippers, and that we performed animal sacrifices as well as drug-induced séances. In truth, we do not give any thought to Satan at all, allowing him no place of residence in our consciousness. We have a "no drug" policy, and most of us are primarily vegetarian. Even the fish in our pond are pets, and we greet them in the morning during breakfast on the dock, feeding them bread.

Seeing this as an opportunity to unite and bring clarity regarding who we were, thus clearing up any misunderstandings, I invited them to come. At the time there was a woman named Tammy and a few other guests downstairs having coffee and tea. When I informed them of the folks that were coming, I saw a look of fear and discomfort in their eyes. I told them not to worry; the ministers are just people and put their pants on one leg at a time like everyone else. Despite my advice, our guests packed up and Tammy suddenly had somewhere else to go.

Soon after everyone left, a parade of cars began to move up the winding driveway lined with ponderosa pines I'd previously planted. They were my sentinels, and I seemed connected to them in some way, for I always knew when someone was coming up the driveway. I took a deep breath, said a prayer for Spirit to watch over me and give me the proper words to serve the highest and best good of all, and went to greet the ministers.

Luckily my guests had left just enough coffee and tea, and I invited the new visitors in to discuss the nature of the meeting. One of the ministers said, "We want to understand where you are coming from, just what you believe in."

I told them, "We believe much like you. We believe in universal peace, brotherly/sisterly love, individual freedom and prosperity for all, with a strong reverence for life."

One of the ministers asked me point-blank, "Do you accept Jesus Christ as your personal lord and savior?"

I told him, "My relationship with Jesus is between me and Jesus, and not something to boast about to the world. If you truly knew Jesus, you would know me, and the question would have already been answered."

Rather than going within, he again asked, "Why can't you declare Jesus Christ as your personal lord and savior?"

I told him, "There is a passage where Jesus says, 'Do not call me master, for the servant does not know what the master is doing; henceforth call me friend.'"

Jesus to me is a brother and friend. I do not believe in making him responsible for my choices and actions, nor do I blame or give credit to GOD for everything. I think that it is time we all take responsibility for our attitudes, emotions and actions that create our tomorrow.

Another minister asked me if I believed Jesus was GOD in the flesh. I told him, "Yes, everything and everyone is GOD. GOD is the one consciousness that encompasses all consciousness on all planes and dimensions throughout the multiverses. The Creator is omnipresent within all Creation."

The first minister asked why I could not accept Jesus as GOD. I told him, "I just did, yet I do not separate Jesus or GOD, nor you nor I from omnipresence."

I then asked him a question: "If Jesus was GOD, whom did he incessantly pray to while on Earth?" There was silence.

I asked him again, "Who were the celestial sons of God referred to in Genesis, and why is Elohim, the name of God, plural?" Again there was silence.

Another minister said, "I hear you people channel."

I told him "Is it not written that there shall come a day when angels will descend upon men and speak through men? We are fulfilling a prophecy."

He responded with another question about how New Age people think they are Gods. I asked him, "What happens when the children of God grow up?" I paraphrased Meister Eckhart, a Christian theologian who said, "If pear seeds produce pear trees and nuts produce nut trees, what do God seeds produce?" I then quoted several passages in the Bible where it is written that man/woman are created in the same image and likeness of God. Ye are all Gods, children of the most high. The light that lighteth every man/woman is the light of God, and the Temple of God is within.

Another minister asked, "Do you believe in reincarnation?"

I told him, "No, I do not *believe* in reincarnation. I *know* reincarnation exists, and I am in full knowledge of many of my past lives. I am also aware of the afterlife, where the eternal soul goes once it leaves this physical expression, and I have stood before the Source Itself. This is not passed-down book knowledge—this is firsthand experience. Reincarnation was taken out of the Bible by the Second Council of Constantinople, because they did not want people to think that they had endless opportunities to evolve. They wanted people to get it right in one lifetime. This is common knowledge, and well known among Bible historians.

Reincarnation was part of the Essene beliefs of which Jesus was a part. There were a couple of passages left in the Bible that the council missed. One is, 'No one ascends into heaven but he who comes from heaven, even the son of man.' Another passage is when Jesus says, 'John is Elijah, who was to come.' Elijah preceded John in history, and returned as John the Baptist. I do not know how this can be interpreted in any way other than reincarnation."

The local minister stood up and said, "You will never get us to give up our belief in Jesus. It is written very clearly that he is the way, and no one will enter Heaven but through him."

I told him, "I never asked you to give up your belief in Jesus, or change in any way. I am just providing clarity and an opportunity to see Jesus in a greater light. Before Jesus said, 'I AM the way, the truth and the light, and no man shall enter Heaven but through me,' he said, 'I of myself do nothing; the Father through me doeth the works.' Now, we have to ask ourselves, who was speaking? Was it GOD speaking through Jesus who said I AM the way, or was it the personality Jesus speaking?

"Another question is, do we worship the man, the personality Jesus, or the GOD speaking through Jesus? The removal of references to reincarnation and the belief that Jesus is the only way one can enter Heaven, along with the Bible being the only written word of GOD is in error. GOD, having no other messengers for other cultures, or children for that matter, has been the foundation for the crusades, the inquisitions, and endless holy wars.

"More have died in the name of GOD than have ever been saved. To separate into structured truths and then judge, condemn and war upon others who do not accept your names, images and doctrines, has nothing to do with universal peace or brotherly/sisterly love, the foundation for true Christianity. It has everything to do with the desires of men for power and control.

"In the very near future, we are going to have to make

a choice of whether we serve GOD or an institution. It will be interesting to find out which side of the fence we will be sitting on when that day comes. The GOD I love has the capacity to love all people and all life. There are no divisions in GOD, there is no separation in omnipresence, the Creator is omnipresent within all Creation, and as Paul said, 'When you are walking in love, you are walking with GOD.'"

On that note, the ministers rose and thanked me for my time. Several said they found the message very interesting, and had some reading to do. I invited them back anytime to discuss the matter further.

A trail of dust followed them as they made their way down the road. I knew a greater force was with me, speaking through me. I looked up to the sky and said, "Thank you GOD, and thank you Jesus and any other Master who threw in their two cents."

A wonderful blessing sent chills down my spine. I heard, "You have done well, my son." My eyes began to water with tears of joy. I hoped that somehow I had reached those ministers, and they in turn would reach others. Thus far, not one has returned to the center, yet in my heart of hearts, I know seeds were planted.

Enslaved through Dependency

Living in the mountains, I could see clearly how much we are enslaved through dependency. I could also see how sovereignty and independence are a direct threat to our government that, ironically, was founded on independence.

I read a Y2K report by the President's Commission and it said that the government is very concerned about those who are becoming independent and sovereign and who are preparing for a breakdown in the system. A government that is there to serve the people, and which was founded on independence, should welcome and support the move towards independence and sovereignty. In truth, ultimately they depend on your dependency. What happens if you do not need them; if you wake up one day and see you can do much better without them?

There are many factors that can cause a breakdown in the present system. The Y2K computer bug, where in the year 2000, computers have a nervous breakdown, lock up and stop operating, spitting out incorrect data, was one. This did not turn out to be a major event.

A stock market crash or economic disaster is another. There are natural disasters such as hurricanes, tornadoes, super storms, flooding, and droughts and freezes creating food shortages. There are also earthquakes, tsunamis and volcanic eruptions.

The most overlooked and likely event is a CME, a coronal mass ejection, or flare from the Sun. We are entering into the greatest solar storm activity in recorded history, referred to by scientists as a mega cycle. The Sun is like a revolving cannon, firing one plasma blast after another, and a direct hit is inevitable. This would knock out both the communications and power grids. Most of our satellites would sustain massive surges, short-circuiting them. ATMs, pagers, cell phones, radio and TV stations would all go down.

Have you ever wondered how independent you are, and what would happen if the lifelines were cut? What about the gas lines, water lines, power and communication grid? Go out one day and flip the main breaker, shut off the gas and water and see what happens. Try living a few days off the grid.

Our remote mountain retreat center has had many opportunities to experience life without utilities. One winter, the main highway was washed out. There was no way in or out for two weeks. We lost our power as well, because the power lines went down with the highway.

Another time the power shorted at the pole, and we had no electricity for two weeks. Actually, the candles and quiet reminded me of a monastery, and it was rather enjoyable. We have a wood stove for heat and a wood cook stove in the kitchen for cooking our meals. Our water heater was electric, however, leaving us without showers and baths. We often jockeyed for positions upwind from each other.

In the summer it does not matter, because we have a large pond and a river. We installed a propane water heater, and now all the basics are covered. If the power goes out, we light a couple of lanterns and candles, or go to bed and rise with the Sun.

Some people would go nuts losing their TV for a day. But there is nothing like a long walk on a star-filled night, or greeting the Sun with a morning meditation. Learning to play an instrument like a flute, guitar or drums is always fun. Campfires brighten up the evening in many ways. The simplest things often bring the most enjoyment and have lasting memories.

There were times when I would look at the large cities with people rushing everywhere, bumper-to-bumper traffic, fighting over parking places, etc. I would wonder, what would happen if the utility lines went down? What would people do? They could run to the supermarket for supplies, but there would be no way to cook or preserve the food. The refrigerator would not work and the microwave would be out. The electric stove would be useless. How about the gas? Could they keep the pressure up with no electricity? Could they pump the water to you and the sewage away from you? With no water, what happens when you cannot flush your toilet or the pee traps dry up, causing the sewers to vent inside the house? Just the sewers backing up or methane venting inside the house would be enough to move you out. Sooner or later, someone would light a match.

What would happen if the gas stations could not pump gas? The freeways would become a gridlock, because people would run out of gas or could not get off them, due to traffic light failures.

I would often ponder the way this civilization has set up their cities and why. How fragile city life is when compared to nature. Cities are all about dependency—dependency on the mega oil and utility companies. I wonder who will be to blame when the lifelines fail, especially since we have had free energy beginning in the 1940s for our utility and transportation needs.

In a dream, I was shown how I was to teach and create a working example of sovereign, self-sufficient living, a spiritual life in harmony with nature, not warring against it. This dream turned out to meet much more resistance than I ever imagined. As long as money was the manifesting force behind destiny, and profit and greed were in charge, I knew I would find little support from the mainstream, especially when people's survival, security and acceptance depended upon them marching to the tune of social consciousness.

Lama Gyatrul Rinpoche

I was feeling a strong call to Tibet. I knew I had had many past lives there, living in the monasteries. There is a strong presence or wisdom coming from Tibet that I felt I could always tap into from within, and I was feeling that it was time to reconnect in my soul to my Tibetan heritage. What was strange was, whenever I felt the need to travel to India or Tibet, a yogi or lama just seemed to appear in the physical or in my meditations.

Lama Gyatrul Rinpoche was appearing to me the second way, though I did not know who he was at first. One of my students in the Inner Sensitivity and Intuitional Training classes came and told me she had a lama she studied with, and she wanted me to meet him. I knew as soon as she brought up the subject that I was to meet him very soon.

When I went to meditate on this, my teeth began to buck out, and a man in orange robes appeared in front of me clairvoyantly. It was very strange, but I still did not put two and two together.

I went to meet Lama Rinpoche in Portland, where he was initiating people into the Tibetan spiritual tradition. When he saw me, he pointed to his teeth; they were, with all due respect, a bit protruding. I know he is listening to my thoughts, so I will have to say what a good-looking guy he is. I sure don't want to create any karma and be born in the next life with buckteeth.

The lama started jumping up and down in excitement when I talked about the center I was building; he knew how important it was. His closest students said he had never gotten excited like that before, so what I am doing must be incredibly important.

After my initiation by him, I was given my dharma name, which is Rigdzin Norbu. When translated, it means "Jewel of Pure Awareness." I was deeply honored, and I prayed I would live up to the task that was set before me.

There comes a time on the road to enlightenment when you have to evaluate your sanity. His endorsement meant everything in the world to me. To this day, I look at the card I was given, and it inspires me to go forward.

Blaji the Pleiadian

My first contact with Blaji, a female ET, though blissful in one sense, was very unnerving to my ego, to say the least. I was on a spiritual journey, and off-world visitors were not my focus. What I did not understand is that you cannot truly comprehend our ancient past in any religion until you understand the nature of these ancient, off-world entities that have been with us since the beginning of time. Most of them are benevolent, and some are our ancient ancestors. There were also those who abused their intellectual and technological superiority, passing themselves off as Gods. This is where the concept of the wrathful God originated, and it is covered extensively in my first book, *Reunion with Source.*

These self-centered, technologically-advanced, yet spiritually-backward tyrants took advantage of primitive people, using fear, guilt and unworthiness to separate Earth humanity from their divinity, forcing them in many cases into slavery. The benevolent, spiritually-advanced ETs would often come back, kick the negative ETs out, and try to repair the damage. Often they would teach and inspire great Masters within the various cultures to bring a message of universal peace, brotherly/sisterly love, and other universal principles and understandings necessary for a healthy society and environment. These benevolent ETs are hundreds, thousands, and some even millions of years ahead of Earth in the time flow, as we know it. They have been with us for eons as inspirational overseers.

Blaji is one such overseer. She is a Pleiadian master spiritual teacher who is here to assist humanity into a higher evolution, incorporating love as the manifesting force behind creation.

My first experience with Blaji was during an all-day meditation. I was deep in trance, feeling ecstatic bliss, when a stream of higher consciousness and energy began to flow into me. There was a telepathic conversation which concerned the awakening and healing process underway on Earth, and what humanity needs to do to assist in cleaning up the consciousness and environment. I was certain at the time that the information was originating from a very high source, due to its content, and I asked what level or dimension it was from. The answer I received threw me for a loop. The transmission came in loud and clear: "We are on a ship."

I quickly ended the meditation, rose to my feet, and said to myself, "Well James, now you have really lost it." I attributed the experience to an overactive imagination, and decided to go out into the garden and get grounded. I was still feeling higher than a kite, due to the spiritual energies I'd been engaging. Before I made it to the front door, my sister and a friend ran up the porch steps and began banging on the door. They said, "Did you see it? Did you see it?"

I said, "See what?" They told me there was a metallic ship, glistening in the Sun and hovering just above the house. Now I had to own the fact that I was being contacted by a very spiritually advanced race of ETs.

Blaji the Pleiadian

Blaji's teachings were impeccable, and were demonstrated in a variety of ways. She would often take me out-of-body to a higher frequency to give me firsthand experience.

Once I was in mid-stride, walking down a country road. I was taken out-of-body for what seemed to be a week, where I went through intense training and indoctrination. I was then brought back in mid-stride, not losing even a second in Earth time. There was a brief moment as I came into awareness when I shifted from that other reality to this one, and the transition made me spacey. It caused me to stumble for a second, yet when I returned I had a whole different perspective about life and many of the problems I was facing. The reason I had taken the walk in the first place was to clear my head in hopes of finding some answers to a few problems.

In another experience, I found myself on a Pleiadian ship, beamed aboard it in what seemed to be a physical experience, and was given a tight blue jumpsuit that fit perfectly. It was invigorating just to wear it, for it had energy of its own. We were soon hovering just in front of a fire-watch tower in the woods. I was looking at the frightened people there who were scurrying around at first, but who were soon calmed down by the loving presence of the Pleiadians.

These ETs have the ability to spiritually and technologically transmit peaceful loving energies to those they are contacting, in order to negate our standard fears of the unknown. The occupants of the fire tower settled down, and one began to sketch the ship. I could see that this was part of the contact scenario, a way of breaking in the people little by little as to the ET presence.

I later saw another dramatic picture. The same man I had observed in the fire tower, while on the ship, went on "Town Hall," a local TV show, and told his story. I was watching the program at the time, and about fell out of my chair. I ran through the house telling everyone, "That's him, the man I saw while on the ship!" The event had a dual purpose: It corroborated my experience and brought awareness to people as to the reality of UFOs.

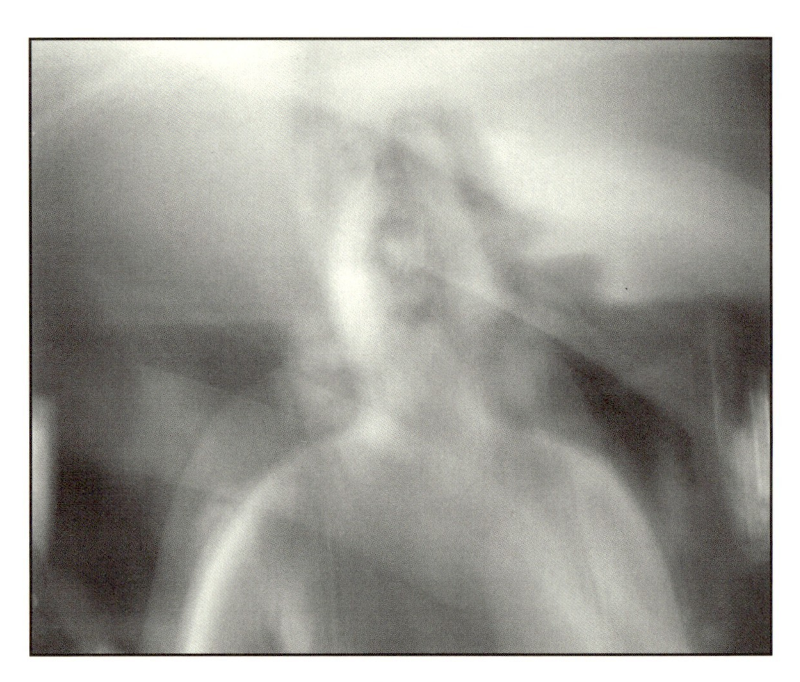

James going out-of-body in a meditation

3

More UFO Sightings

UFO sightings began to be a part of my everyday life. I never cared about proving the existence of UFOs; for me it was an inward experience. One day in meditation I was told it was time to bring it out into the open; they would provide undeniable video footage of their ships.

The following week, a man named Choi appeared at author Randolph Winters' lecture at the center. Choi tried to leave twice but came back in, telling me he could not leave, because there was something here that he had to do or know. He said he had studied in all the mystery schools in the East and there was still a missing element: a baffling connection to UFOs throughout each teaching he had studied. It was ancient, and no one could tell him who they were and what the connection was. I said to him, "Rather than me tell you, why don't we let them tell you?"

We took him through a process of removing any blocks or patterns that would get in the way of him making his own contact. At the end of the process, Haog, a master teacher from the Orion Council of Light, came in and communicated. Choi was overwhelmed with the energies. In his own words, he said it was "10,000 times stronger" than anything he had ever experienced from any other master. This was a real compliment, for he had studied with the best and was a master himself in kung fu, qi gong and several other forms of martial arts and meditation techniques.

What we did not know is that he had a $7,000 video

camera. He was told during contact with the Pleiadians to take the camera on the plane during his journey to Los Angeles the following week. He called us and told us he was getting a message to film them. He said, "I feel like I am going crazy, or it is my imagination?" I asked Blaji telepathically if this message to take the camera on the plane was correct, and she acknowledged it was. I then called Choi and told him to take the camcorder on the trip. He said, "I think I am going crazy; it is like a voice in my head."

I told him, "Take the camera, and if they do not show up, then you are crazy." I knew, however, that the Pleiadians would make good on their promise.

The Burn Pile Incident

Choi was extremely excited now. His dreams and long search for the understandings concerning the spiritual and ancient connection of UFOs with Earth had finally come to fruition. His courage and tenacity in seeking out the truth had been unsurpassed. Yet even his extensive training in martial arts, qi gong and spiritual discipline was not enough for the next encounter.

We often say we want to know: We want proof, we want to see them face-to-face. What we really have to ask ourselves is, are we truly ready? When it comes down to full-blown contact, most people, despite their assertions, are not ready. Contact must happen a little at a time, so as to avoid creating fear and shocking the ego or personality self, developed while living on Earth. There is also much programming from Hollywood as to the negative nature of ETs—seeking humans and sticking apples in their mouths, cooking them well-done with an enormous laser, sucking out their brains, vaporizing entire cities, switching human heads with animal heads, etc. Then there is the religious programming that says that everything that is not God or an angel is the devil; even the devil himself can appear as an angel.

This covers all the bases, to keep those in authority as the dictators of your experience. There is also the basic fear of the unknown. Fear in its many forms is greatly amplified in the presence of the benevolent and spiritually advanced ETs, and they have to hold the contactees in a field of love to assist them in overcoming these fears. Then they have to bring the contactees along a little at a time, teaching them the truth about ETs, their connection to the Earth as our ancient ancestors, and little by little, dismantle all the recycled ignorance we have been taught within the mainstream religious and educational systems. This retraining can come as quite a shock if given all at once, for the ego is very fragile.

A classic example happened one evening, with skies so clear it looked like you could reach out and grab a star. We had just had rain, and the timing was perfect. I decided to burn a large pile of tree limbs, rotten wood, etc. It was quite a large fire, so intense that we could not get within 20 feet of it. There were enormous dancing flames of yellow and orange, and billowing smoke rising high into the late-night sky.

Choi asked over and over for the ETs to bring a ship down. He said, "I will come forward and speak on their behalf, carrying the message around the world, if they just come down lower. They have to show me metallic craft; do something that proves beyond a shadow of a doubt that they are real."

I asked Choi if he really thought he was ready. We often think we are ready, yet when it comes to the ships dropping down low, many people scream, "Oh my God!" as they head for the nearest cover, and panic and fear takes over. This is exactly what the benevolent ETs are trying to avoid. They scan the people's consciousness, and if fear is present, they stay high in the heavens or do not appear at all.

Choi got really excited and said, "I am ready. Please tell them I will do anything—just bring the ship down."

I told him, "Why go through me? Tell them yourself. You have the same contact I do; they will hear you." Right after my words, I felt a strong presence behind me coming in from the south. I told Choi, "They are here," and turned around, pointing to the south. When I did so, three ships appeared, moving directly towards us. As the ships approached, one dropped out of formation and gently and silently glided down right over our heads. It hovered for about 30 seconds, then rose up to join the other two, all moving off in a long, wide turn, back from where they had come. I began laughing as they faded into the distance.

Choi snapped out of a frozen stance and refocused his eyes, which, along with his mouth, were wide open in awe. He said, "What is so funny?" I pointed to the video camera strapped underneath his arm, which had never moved. Choi became very upset with himself. He said a few words which will not be printed here and which were contrary to his moral character. He then said, "I blew it, I blew it! How could I have been so stupid?" He was really down on himself. I told him to stop being so hard on himself; fear is a perfectly normal reaction. I also told him to give himself credit for coming this far. Most people don't have the courage to ask for full contact, or even the interest in asking.

It took quite a while to calm Choi down and get him to stop beating up on himself. I reminded him that despite all of his martial arts training and his fearless nature, this is no match for the programming of social consciousness that is so deeply ingrained. I also told him, "Remember this experience when dealing with others. It will give you the compassion and understanding necessary to see why people behave the way they do when confronting the unknown. Now you know why it must be a little at a time."

Lessons on Cover-ups and Disinformation

Choi called me immediately after his trip to Los Angeles. He said, "I have a surprise for you." He came up to the center with a video in hand, and sure enough, it was Blaji's ship doing some miraculous aerial displays alongside of the commercial plane Choi was on. Her ship fell from the sky as a metallic disk, moving from side to side. It stabilized, then turned into a golden white light with orange coming from beneath the ship. It then began to shape-shift from a disk to a cylinder, then an arrowhead, followed by the image of a hand, then back to a disk of light. It is an awesome video, and makes one wonder just who these people are and how long they have been around, overseeing our evolution.

We quickly sent the footage out to various UFO groups and were in for a shocking experience: Most of the copies of the tape mysteriously disappeared. Some were diverted during shipping and altered to worsen the sound or picture quality.

Soon we had visits from black helicopters flying above the center on a regular basis; choppers with elaborate gear on them. Some had threc C-shaped tubes on the front; others had dishes and other high-tech gear. They did several intimidation runs to let us know they knew about the video. One time, they flew so low that I could see a mole on the pilot's face. The crew was wearing light brown or tan-colored overalls with an insignia on the front. The helicopters had no markings whatsoever.

On one occasion I grabbed my camcorder and ran out in the north field as a black helicopter was approaching the Sanctuary. My friends thought I was crazy, like a madman rushing into battle. As the helicopter vectored in on the main lodge, I was there to greet it. At first you could only hear it, yet there was nothing in sight. It came very close before it became visible, as if it was cloaked. When it appeared overhead, I noticed another diamond-shaped object hovering inbetween the helicopter and myself. It was as if they were standing guard inbetween us, insuring my safety. When reviewing the video a warm feeling came over me, an inner feeling of peace, knowing that I was protected.

I asked Shari, a friend of mine with the UFO group CSETI, about the black helicopters, and she said they carry ultra-sensitive scanning and psychotronic warfare equipment on them. They can sedate you, make you angry, and even trigger retroviruses in the body, causing severe illness and sometimes even cancer, heart attacks or death. I was also told of other UFO investigators who were all coming down with the same form of cancer. I really did not want to believe her; I was hoping she was wrong. She died of cancer shortly thereafter, which was a great loss to the UFO community. She stood for truth and universal peace, her courage was noted by many, and she is sorely missed.

Soon after the videos were sent out, Choi came down with a mysterious disease. His body broke out in lesions that covered him from head to toe, as if he had been nuked by some form of energy. He said he felt as though he had been microwaved. He was having shortness of breath and chest pains, and was in fear for his life. He called and told us he felt that if he went into the hospital, he would not come out.

I had a friend pick him up and bring him to the center. We used some Native American remedies on him, filled him with barley soup to help detoxify him, and used some energetic healing on him. We also contacted Blaji and told her what had happened. I felt it was due to helping her get the message out that this had occurred, and I asked her if she could assist him. He was up and around the next day, the lesions had almost vanished, and it was like a miracle.

This event was too much for him, and he is no longer associated with us. He was called into the immigration office and told that his school visa suddenly had a problem with it. Basically, he was sent back to Korea.

I do not blame him for going back to his country and not contacting us anymore, yet I do miss him as a good friend. I was saddened that this happened to a friend, and I felt somewhat responsible. I was very determined now to get the message out. It was a strong message concerning upcoming changes in the land and in consciousness—how we have to get our consciousness and environment in order. I also described ways to assist in the awakening and healing of humanity and the Earth.

I continued to mail out copies of the video, and was surprised at how many of the people we all know and trust in the UFO community were not what they seemed. Many suppressed or censored the video and the contacts happening at the Sanctuary. Many had NSA, CIA, and military intelligence backgrounds, yet were the heads of certain UFO reporting centers and groups. There were also politics, positions to maintain, envy and competition for money involved. Some were in it just for the notoriety.

Many groups wanted to keep capitalizing on fear and suspense; they wanted to push the negative encounter agenda, ignoring all other facets of contact. Other groups wanted to have their truth as the only truth, and would not allow any contacts to come forward that did not square with their belief system. Many groups are nuts-and-bolts, and do not acknowledge the fact that an advanced civilization would also be advanced in consciousness. However, the ETs would have to balance out their technology with spirituality or they would eventually do themselves in like other Earth civilizations did before ours.

I had no idea of the barriers that would come before me; nonetheless I continued. I was partially fueled by what had been done to my friends. I had already died once anyway, so what the heck.

The UFOs continued to fly overhead, and eventually there were so many eyewitnesses that the truth had to come forward. I would tell the debunkers at lectures, "Rather than me prove it to you, come up and see it yourself." They would not come, yet others in the audience would, and return home grinning and wide-eyed, with a testimony putting the scoffers to shame.

One of the greatest breakthroughs was with Jeff Rense, the host of the radio show "Sightings." He received a copy of the tape that was sent by FedEx; he was supposed to sign for it, yet that copy too was diverted. The people at the wrong address it was sent to delivered it to him, however. He soon had me on his show, followed by several other appearances. He has my deepest respect. This launched the beginning of getting the message out, and was supplemented by eyewitness testimonies too numerous to document.

Soon afterward, the black helicopters stopped flying over us. What was interesting was that a few months later we were visited by white helicopters—same kind, same gear.

Black helicopter flying over Sattva Sanctuary

Censorship by Death

I had known about the death of many people who got too close to the truth, or too close to some of the back-engineered ships. I had seen what they did to Choi and Shari. I had felt their radionic and psychotronic attacks late at night when I was sleeping. It was like being nuked by microwaves. There were times when we knew we were being subjected to waves of energies designed to create nausea and memory loss and trigger us into anger, trying to create dissension among the group.

Being extremely sensitive, I knew what they were up to and was well trained in dealing with unwanted negative energies. I followed one stream of energy back to a man dressed in black, sitting in a recliner by a whole bank of computers, with apparatus attached to him. They were doing a form of technological black magic or voodoo. They would use this device to plant images and nightmares, and disrupt your sleep patterns. In the worst-case scenario, they could send the frequency pattern of a heart attack or cancer.

I was amazed at what our tax dollars were financing, and how this black technology was being used, not in the interest of national security, but on the very citizens who paid for it. To me this was the ultimate treason, an unlawful and cowardly act. I asked several friends trained in remote viewing to look into the energies being directed towards me and the Sanctuary and they came up with the same information, down to minute details.

There were also several attempts made on my life by sabotaging my truck. Wheels and rims would mysteriously fall off on the highway. Luckily, there was a time on one occasion where I felt it coming and started to slow down, only to be passed by my left front tire. The truck slammed down onto the pavement, cutting a deep groove in the road. My vehicle swerved from side to side, grinding down the front rotor, and eventually came to a stop. I was not worried so much for my own life, but what if I had had my daughter, nieces or nephews with me? I often take them to school or pick them up.

It seems that these black ops boys have no respect for life. I often wonder how they would feel if it were their family. Do they go home and say, "Hi honey, how are the kids? I just wiped out a family like ours today. I created two heart attacks and several cancers. Broke up several families, financially destroyed the lives of a few good citizens and drove several people nuts. It is all in a day's work, in the interest of national security."

I think they were amazed to see me recover over and over. It was as if their nasty toys were not working. What they did not know was that their toys were working; I was deathly ill several times. However, Spirit had more for me to do, and it seemed to heal and lift me up at the last moment.

Although the black ops people think they are very clever, there is one thing they have missed. I've heard a saying: "There is a universal truth, and the eyes of justice are upon you." In the last days, they will have to feel all the pain, suffering and loss they imposed upon others; it is built into the destiny, evolution and vibrational lifting of the Earth. If they were really clever, they would come clean and redirect their energies towards the awakening and healing process.

With all of their psychics and remote viewers they have come to realize one thing in viewing the future: They are not in it. They do not know why, and cannot see themselves beyond 2012. This is because they are not there; they could not make the jump. There is always forgiveness, even for them.

Their time is short, for a greater power will soon be upon them. If they think that their technology is awesome, wait until the ones with the full use of creational energies make their presence known. The wrongdoers will see a band of energy never before experienced on the Earth, and it will bend all of their deeds inward. Those who have chosen to serve humanity and the Earth will be exalted. Those who choose to control, dominate and act at the expense of humanity and the Earth will reap what they have sown.

Haog's Ship

One evening, Choi was filming out the window of his dorm room after receiving a telepathic message. A very large ship from Orion appeared, and it was hovering over Portland State University. It was emitting a tone and pulse that was recorded on the video footage. We took the video to Jim Delettoso with Village Labs, and after analyzing the film, he said there was no evidence of a hoax. He later did some work on the sound to edit out the voices in the background. The deep, low, repetitive hum, followed by a higher faster hum, sounds remarkably like the sound in the movie "Contact." This tape was put into a computer file and sent out around the world.

Not long after Choi did the taping, we asked Haog why the Orion ship was there and he said, "Higher learning." In the sleep and dream state, students were receiving higher knowledge and being prepared for contact. This way it will not be such a shock later when the ships appear.

I also asked him about the steady audible deep tone coming from the ship that pulsed faster when the ship lit up. He said, "It is the tones and pulses of Creation. We have full use of the creational energies, and I am responsible for the energies not becoming too out of balance on Earth." He explained to me the nature of the Earth's grid system, and how infusions of energy were needed to maintain and balance it during the awakening and healing process.

He also showed me the vibrational lifting process, how it worked and how greatly we were loved, as well as how hard the ETs were working on our behalf. Despite ourselves and our desire to war on everything, including our environment, they continue to help us move forward, insuring our evolution.

I remembered some of my earlier readings where the people from Orion were considered to be similar to the grays and the reptilians, and given a bad rap. This did not jive with our experience, which showed them to be extremely advanced, loving and similar to us in appearance, only more Nordic-looking. I found out later that their ancestors were the same as those of the Pleiadians.

I was instructed to read *The Book of Knowledge: The Keys of Enoch,* by J.J. Hurtak. Orion, according to Hurtak, is where the pure light bodies came from that were encoded with the genetic codes of the Pleiades. It was where gnosis, the spiritual powers and knowledge of the Source Itself, originated.

There were many ships flying over the center. There were the usual light disks, there were large golden egg-shaped ships from Sirius A, and there were also the gigantic triangular ships, bigger than cities, from the Andromedas.

One day an Andromedan ship flew over at treetop level. It was a large, triangular ship, measuring at least 100 yards across, with a white light on each corner and a red one in the middle. As it floated over me, it made no noise whatsoever. It flashed a bank of red lights at the rear as it passed. Something that large, and totally silent, seemed unbelievable. It was quite an education, and I had to readjust my ideas of reality.

Reverse Speech

A gentleman asked one day if I had ever taken a lie detector test or had my information checked out with reverse speech. I told him no, yet I was willing to take any tests concerning the matter of whether or not I was telling the truth. I was asked to go on the David John Oates show. He is a renowned master in reverse speech. Reverse speech analyzes what is in your subconscious mind before your conscious mind has a chance to filter and twist the information. It reveals your true feelings and ideas of whatever subject matter is being discussed. It is an excellent method for discerning whether or not someone is telling the truth and revealing any hidden agendas. It is also a wonderful method of getting to one's deep core issues, wounds and traumas that have not yet been addressed and healed.

When asked to come on the show I said, "Sure, why not? I have nothing to hide and have been telling the truth all along." Then I began to think about it for a while. Worry started to set in. My mind started coming up with all kinds of fears. What if it was all an illusion and I was being somehow used in some bizarre plot? What if their equipment is not for real, and they just make up things to debunk true sightings and contacts? What if I have some deep emotional issues that are going to be aired to all on national radio?

I sat with my fears until they faded away, then said to myself, "So what? I need to know if there is anything hidden in my own subconscious and if I am fooling myself. How can I ask others to come forward and face this issue if I shrink with fear?" The butterflies in my stomach vanished, and I did the radio show. There was a man named Jon Kelly who also did reverse speech. They worked together on recorded interviews, and what was amazing is that I was saying the same thing in reverse that I was saying in regular speech, only I was revealing even more information that was held within my subconscious.

When asked about the Mary connection and her appearance at the Sanctuary and some of the interactions, several messages came out in reverse speech. One said, "With Mary, preservation is assured." Another said, "Mary's elves say to love her." This was a real shocker because there were little energy beings that gathered around her, and I have had a lot of fleeting visions of elves on the property. The kids saw them, and described them in detail.

When I was talking about the large, golden ships that frequently appear at the center, I said these ships have a very ancient feel to them and have been around for a long, long time. When reversed I said, "Sailor Vishnu is his name." I about fell out of my chair, because Vishnu is the ancient Hindu God of preservation.

These great ships are also found in ancient sacred books of Tibet and India. The Vedic literature, the Mahabharata and the Ramayana give in-depth descriptions of four ships: the Rukma, Sundara, Tripura, and the Sakuma. They were the chariots of the Gods and had very advanced weaponry on board. Some of the ships were physical, some were more of an energy or plasma ship, and some were created by the spiritual energies of the occupants. Sound-seeking and heat-seeking fiery arrows and whirling disks were fired from these ships.

There is documentation of a great war in ancient times, and upon excavation of the site where this war was written to have been waged, at the exact level of ground dated to match the written documentation, it was found to be radioactive. When I showed the pictures of the large, golden plasma ships that appear in the sky over the Sanctuary to Lamas and Yogis, they jump up and get all excited, calling them Vimanas, or the chariots of the Gods. The golden ships are recorded undeniably in the ancient Vedic literature. They were the chariots of the Gods. I knew now that I was on to something...something very ancient and very big.

Crop Circles

I asked Haog and my Pleiadian friends about the nature of crop circles. The antics of Doug and Dave, two drunken Englishmen who said they went out late at night after a few beers and made the crop circles, did not explain all the circles. One has only to look at a typical circle to see that it would have taken a whole team of engineers, surveyors and helicopters to make a crop circle as complex as the ones being created, and leave no footprints.

There were a few hoaxed ones and one that was created by a crew for network television, yet these are easily dismissed as fakes due to the evidence left behind. The crop was broken and trampled, not laid down and woven. It was full of footprints and took quite a long time to do.

The real crop circles often baffled the experts. They demonstrated a very high understanding of science and geometry, were extremely complex, very large, and they were formed within moments, not hours or days. Planes would fly over the area, make a turn, then come back, and the circle was there. The crop was interwoven and bent, not broken, by some form of energy resembling microwaves. Even the soil underwent changes, and there were magnetic anomalies as well. I knew there was an intelligence far beyond ours that was making the circles.

Haog told me that the circles represented the key to creational energies. They are very complex by our standards, and they will be deciphered soon in our future. They have not one, but many, meanings. Some represent a divine science known as sacred geometry, and depict different phases of Creation, taking something from its lowest and simplest form into more complex forms. They will be the keys to understanding the levels of Creation—planes, dimensions and how to think in a more infinite, rather than a finite, manner.

Infinity goes in both directions; we can get infinitely small or infinitely large, which is beyond the comprehension of most people. You will find as you go out into space that this solar system is just one of many. There are ten billion suns in our Milky Way alone, with planets revolving around them.

Moreover, this galaxy is just one of many. There is galaxy after galaxy, each unique with its solar systems, stars and planets. There is universe after universe, containing these galaxies with their solar systems. Creation is infinite; it has no beginning, and no ending. It goes within and without, like the breath, and every little fraction of it contains the information of the whole. Everything is connected, and communicates instantaneously through this connection.

The crop circles are keys to this understanding. These keys were known in the past by our ancient ancestors, and were used in the building of their temples. You will find that many of the symbols found within the circles are also found in these ancient temples. These ancestors, many of whom have gone interdimensional, are returning now. The veils are getting thinner and thinner, and soon almost all will know of their existence.

In the most limited understanding, the crop circles are greeting cards, telling the people of Earth to look up, expand their horizons, and go within, because there is much more here than meets the physical eye. There are multiverses, with all their planes and dimensions filled with life, some vastly older and more intelligent than our own civilization. It is time to join the rest of Creation.

I asked Haog to be a little more specific about how the crop circles are done. I knew we would lose the nuts-and-bolts people with a metaphysical explanation. He said, "It is done very simply. We release a probe. The probe has the pattern programmed into it; it zips along the ground at light speed, laying down the pattern. That is one way it is done. There are other groups with other ways." This explains the little orange balls of light that are often seen speeding around before the crop circle manifests.

4

Meeting Mastors and Off-World Beings

The Hators

I was fast asleep one night, and in a dream I was being taught concerning the nature of tones, sounds and vibrational healing. When I awoke, I saw a woman standing at the foot of my bed. She was not like anything I had ever seen; her face was triangular and her ears were not like human ears, but were more like the ears of a cow, only smaller. She was exquisitely beautiful, and the love coming from her was overwhelming. At first it shocked me to see her. It is not every day that a being appears at the foot of your bed in a form that is totally alien to your consciousness. However, I continued to feel the love and peace emanating from her and I felt very much at ease. I did the usual healing prayer to insure that she was of the light and she smiled, nodding in agreement, and faded away.

The Hators, or Hathors as some would refer to them, continued to appear to me, teaching me lessons concerning the nature and rise of feminine creational energies. Mary was still coming to me, along with Blaji, and I saw how the spiritual evolution of humanity was unfolding.

First the Shekinah feminine energies such as Mary, Buffalo Calf Woman, Quan Yin and other feminine Masters would balance out the patriarchal energies. This would pave the way for Pleiadian contact, followed by the Masters from Orion, Sirius and Arcturus. Then the Andromedan energies would come in; the beings mythologically known as archangels. They have magnetized light bodies that are eight to ten feet tall, and are the true overseers of the multiverses.

I saw how the evolutionary process moved from physical bodies to energy bodies, and then to light bodies along the vibrational continuum. I was also shown how we would become less dense in our own bodies, due to the changes in DNA and the transmutation process.

The Sun would play an important part in the spiritual and physical unfoldment of humanity and the Earth, and it too is not what it seems, as humanity will soon come to realize. The suns govern everything; imagine if our Sun went out. Each sun is connected to a Great Central Sun that governs the evolutionary process of the universe. This is why so many cultures worshipped the Sun. It possesses intelligence far beyond our imagination.

Melia of Orion

Melia began to appear to me when my friend Alice came to visit the center. This Orion woman was her main teacher and guide. I too felt her presence, and it was very loving and powerful in consciousness. We decided to strengthen the link.

When Alice made a full connection with Melia for the first time, the tears of joy were overflowing; it was like finding a long-lost sister. The following evening a golden ship was seen over the ranch. I decided to take a bath that night and meditate. In the meditation I said, "I want to know. I want to know who I am, my off-world lives—full memory, not just a vague vision." A few moments later, a large stream of light hit me in the chest. It was for the purpose of soul activation, to bring forward the ancient memories. Three balls of energy came in on the stream of light and also hit me in the chest.

Melia of the Orion Council of Light

The next moment, I was standing before Melia, who wore a white headdress with two golden bands on it. I was told it was to transfer powerful consciousness and energy for the awakening process. I was also told this would be happening to many people as an initiation, once they reached a certain level of conscious evolution.

I now had a new sense of self, and I became very steadfast and grounded in purpose. I had full memory of being a spiritual teacher on Orion, as well as an Ishrish in the Pleiades, reaching a very high degree of wisdom. I also remembered lives on Earth where I was a prophet, a yogi, a lama, an elder with the Algonquin tribe, and many other lives. I could see I was well prepared for my journey here on Earth, to assist in the awakening and healing of humanity and the Earth. I could understand all faiths, because I had practiced all faiths. I had also experienced the stars.

The Lion People

Upon my being initiated into the memories of my past off-world incarnations, ancient connections began to unfold. One such ancient connection was with the Lion People, or Felines. There is a master race of beings that ascended during a time long since past. They are returning to assist Earth's humanity in its spiritual evolution. As the veils become thinner and people move into awareness of other planes and dimensions, some will come into awareness and contact with ancient civilizations that still exist, but on a different frequency or in a different time.

The contact with the Felines was very brief. My Pleiadian teacher Blaji set up the meeting to expand my understanding of the multiverse, its many dimensions and its myriad inhabitants. I was in awe of the beauty of these beings. I found through research that the Felines are known to many ancient cultures. They are known as Nrishinga, the God of Protection, an incarnation of Vishnu in India;

Sekhmet was also a God of Protection in Egypt, and I am sure they go back even further in time, as we know it. There are many chants in India to Nrishinga, to ask for protection from demons or other negative influences.

The courage of the lion is well known in every culture; match that with the higher wisdom of an advanced ascended civilization, and you have quite an ally. I am looking forward to learning more from this master race. I wish I could convey more information concerning these beings, but they are still very new to me. I do know one thing: They are exquisitely beautiful, bipedal, and look more like humans than cats.

The one I met had long, golden head hair, very short, light gold fur, wore clothing, and was very busy at what looked like a large computer console. When she stood up to greet me, the warmth of her being, her loving eyes and spiritual energies were almost overwhelming. It made me wonder why I was beating my head against the wall of social consciousness with all its discriminations in this civilization, when the heavens seem to have such a myriad of entities which all get along with one another.

The Amethyst Crystal Skull

My meeting with the amethyst skull came about through a series of events. I was told by a friend that there was a woman in Chicago who was having trouble dealing with some unseen negative energies. Being well trained in healing these influences, I was asked to help. I had no idea what I was getting into at the time. The energies were multi-level, with some grey alien influence as well.

Her group had a crystal skull, and was having a lot of difficulty with it and the energies emitting from it. It was a great amplifier, and at times had energies around it that needed healing. When I called her she said, "You are the keeper of the skull," and began to describe me to a tee. The group had had visions of me coming, and was told that the second call would be the one who could help and would be the new keeper of the skull. As the universe would have it, I was the second caller. I had mixed emotions about whether or not I even wanted it.

The energies here at the Sanctuary were very high already, balanced and clear. It is my job to maintain those energies, creating a frequency or vibration that enhances and accelerates the awakening and healing process. I knew the skull seemed to attract energies at times that were not benevolent, yet the group in Chicago could not operate the skull unless they themselves had love and compassion. I found out later through my Pleiadian contacts that it was all right, and part of my destiny to again have the skull. I asked them, "What do you mean by using the word 'again?'"

They said, "You have used it before. It is pre-Atlantis and Lemuria, and is attuned to the Pleiades."

The skull, whose name was Paouli, was delivered by a woman who is a very old soul; it had been sent to her earlier by courier. She and several other women of a very high spiritual nature came to the center bearing their gift. When the skull arrived, I received the same psychokinetic signals from it that I do from my Pleiadian teachers. I was told to bury it as soon as it arrived. I had pre-dug the hole, and as soon as the skull came, I wasted no time in placing it in the ground. We had divined the location earlier and also realized that the land here is full of young amethyst now forming (Paouli is amethyst). I was told later that the skull was a transmitter and receiver of higher consciousness and energy, and it was programming the land. I was also told it needed cleansing itself, and in return, would cleanse the four elements.

After three days we brought Paouli up from the ground. He looked much different; he even glowed with a brilliant golden light that was photographed. We could tell he was really at home and loving the energies here. During the time he was buried, there was a round of quakes near Seattle about 200 miles away.

The next place for Paouli was in the water. We had a

Crystal skull being placed in the water

waterfall on the property, with a swirling pool where he was placed. The following day, swirling clouds began to appear over the Sanctuary, and it began to rain buckets. The land was dry and needed it, yet I have never seen such large drops of water before, coming down so heavy; it seemed very unnatural. Being very grounded and discerning, I put this occurrence on the shelf as interesting.

After the water ceremony we decided to put him out in the air, on top of the deck next to the pyramid. Soon thereafter, the winds began picking up, and there were small whirlwinds everywhere. They even came into the house through the screens. My "interesting" file was getting really big now concerning Paouli, and the events surrounding his arrival.

The last ceremony was the fire ceremony. We decided to build a large fire and put Paouli in front of it at a safe distance. We did a meditation around the fire that night, which was similar to the Tibetan vortex meditations. Towards the end of it, the sky began to light up. A large cloud with a hole in the middle was hovering over the Sanctuary, and it put on what I can only describe as a light symphony—flashes of light moving rapidly through the cloud. There was no lightning or thunder, and the flashing lights seemed to have a guiding intelligence behind them. Everyone was in awe.

Fire is also related to Spirit. It was said in the Bible, "There shall come a great one that will baptize by fire," referring to Jesus. Fire is also related to lightning or electromagnetic energy. Was Paouli using the forces of nature, or was it a visit from on high? I leave the reader to go within for the answer.

Paouli's Sudden Departure

The past owner of "the crystal skull known as Paouli" called and told me she was returning to the Sanctuary. I received information from Cazekiel during meditation that the skull would leave, and not to get attached to it. I was also told that the old owner was going through an identity crisis and that her attachment as keeper and guardian of the skull was too great. She could not release it, because losing the identity of keeper and guardian took away all she had. Paouli had become a crutch, a diversion and distraction from facing her own personal problems. When the crutch was gone, the necessity of facing her issues became overwhelming. Regaining her other identity as keeper and guardian was vital to her ego's survival.

I was told she would do everything to demonize and condemn my work, as well as the work of others at the center, in order to justify taking the skull back. From the moment she set foot on the property, her issues all came forward and were acted out exactly as Cazekiel had warned.

Her constant undermining and projections were very hard to be around. The energies seemed to invade all that was good about the Sanctuary. One evening she came out and confronted me, saying, "You are not the keeper of the skull; I am." She told me she was its true and only guardian. She also told me I was too attached to the skull. She demanded that I inform her of anything that transpired with it immediately. I had to call, fax, etc., any guidance or information coming from the skull.

I waited for her to finish, then told her, "It was talked about in your own words to me and in the presence of others that the skull was to come to me and I was to be the keeper of the skull. Not once, but several times in the presence of others. I did not accept the skull at first. I told you I had to meditate on it, because I had to make sure the problems you were having will not become our problems."

I had also strongly advised her previously, when she was going to take a sledgehammer to the skull and destroy it, not to do so. "It is an amplifier," I had told her. "Bring it here and we will cleanse it." This was accomplished. I reminded her that her group, along with others, had all agreed the crystal skull was to be here at the center.

The last thing I said to her was, "The energy here

amplifies everything, just as the skull does. Your own attachment to the skull as being your claim to fame and identity, is what is being projected. I am not attached to the skull. It is a crystal amplifier and holder of knowledge, yet we are also crystal amplifiers and holders of knowledge, going all the way back to the Source Itself. I do not need a rock to access what is already within. Go and take the skull. It is what your original intention was from the beginning. You do not need to demonize me or the Sanctuary to take it."

The very last thing I told her was, "The skull is different now. It has been amplified even more. It will amplify all of your unhealed energies now, tenfold. This is not a threat; it is just what is."

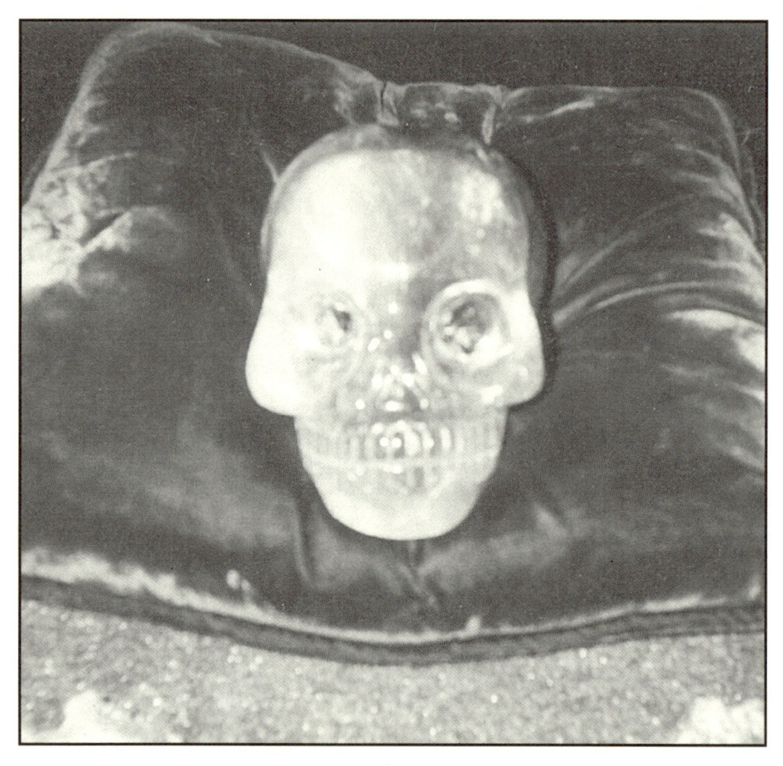

Close-up of crystal skull

She left, taking Paouli with her. She then appointed another keeper who was a friend of mine, making her vow to be silent about the deal and not inform me. The woman she chose had been very involved with the center, and the ownership of the skull now became a wedge between us. The desire for power and recognition outside of self often becomes the means for separation from one's true power within, their own personal God connection, and a distraction from their spiritual path.

A couple of months later, after demanding total subservience and demonizing my friend as she had done to me, the old owner again came and took the skull back to Chicago, locking it in a bank vault. It will be interesting to see what happens in that bank and the city of Chicago.

Paouli enjoyed his stay at the Sanctuary. We had fun playing with the elements. Paouli can only be activated with the right consciousness. His resting place is the Sanctuary, and maybe one day he will return.

As in all experiences, we have a choice. We can greet them as a God or a victim. We can learn by them and heal the past, putting what is in the highest and best good for the people and the planet as first and foremost on our agenda.

Forgiveness is the key; gain the wisdom from the experience, release the charge, and allow it to settle in the soul as wisdom. The battle between ego and spirit is seldom won, yet in the long run Spirit is always the victor. We can only prolong the agony.

Battles in Court and on the Streets

My third court appearance concerning the ongoing extortion of funds was set into motion. I was again served with papers demanding my presence. After a grueling cross-examination by the district attorney, the bottom line was that they had no evidence whatsoever to base their assumptions and accusations upon. All they had was the past false information that was proven once again to be incorrect.

Despite this, the judge ruled that I must pay the lien, even though it was based on fraudulent information, because legal steps had been gone through to create the lien. The DA knew the lien was based on fraudulent data, the welfare department also knew the information was false, and the judge had two previous court documents in his hands, showing beyond a shadow of a doubt that the statistics concerning my job description and income were fabricated. In spite of this, he ruled that I must pay the lien back and get a full-time job where they could garnish my monthly wages. To top it off, being a minister, author, and process-oriented therapist is not a job according to the State of Washington. It is now evident that tyranny and slavery are alive and well here.

At the same time I was doing battle in court, others were doing battle on another front. It was the time of the Seattle WTO meeting. The New World Order, a group of international banking families, the true force behind the mega corporations, and the World Trade Organization decided to have a meeting in Seattle. They were coming together to decide our future, based purely on profit, greed and the perpetuation of their corporations. Many of their plans, as was true in the past, would have disastrous effects on humanity and the Earth.

It seems the people of Seattle and from around the world had a different agenda, and made theirs known as well. Peaceful protesters, many in prayer and meditation, were met with rubber bullets, tear gas, pepper spray and other toxic experimental gases—not to mention the military with oak bats and a varied array of crowd-control weapons. While a very small group of violent protesters got all the press and went ignored by the police, the peaceful protesters were beaten, gassed, and jailed, and experienced many atrocities within the jail itself. This is a wake-up call to show people just how corrupt our system is, and who is in control of the military, the government and even the local police.

Despite the will of the people, the overwhelming majority, the WTO had their meeting. The order to clear the streets came from our very own president. Writing your president or your congressman, or your governor, your mayor or police chief is like writing the wolf to tell the pack it runs with to stop eating your chickens. Yet most people believe that they have a voice, that this is a democracy and our leaders serve the people. However, leaders are governed by the corporations, and it is the corporations that finance the careers of the politicians.

The NWO (New World Order) owns the WTO and the WTO owns the majority of the politicians. Do you think they are there to pass laws in your favor, to stand up for your rights and make sure you have a voice? The ones who are have been publicly or physically assassinated; they seem to have very short careers. Messiahs die young in this day and age.

The protests in Seattle were just the spark of a greater firestorm yet to come. It is part of the process of evolution into higher consciousness. Universal peace, brotherly/sisterly love, equality, individual freedom and prosperity for all, with a strong reverence for life, honoring the sacred circle of life, is coming back, due to popular demand.

It is time to hold our leaders and all governmental, business and religious institutions to these basic principles. Our future depends on it, because if we stay with the present course set by the NWO, WTO and their puppets, this civilization will not survive.

A Healing from a Bushy Haired Yogi

The attacks continued on every level concerning the work I was doing. My truck was sabotaged several more times; there was obviously a game going on. They would sneak up late at night and undo my lug nuts. I would come out and have a feeling something was wrong, check the truck, and find the lug nuts were loosened just enough to come off later when I was driving.

One time I was in a hurry and forgot to check the truck. As I mentioned earlier, the whole rim and tire flew off on the highway. This little mishap cost me hundreds of dollars worth of damage, an expense I had not counted on, leaving me on foot for a while. Loosening lug nuts is one of the standard warnings used by those who would like to keep the UFO cover-up going.

Our sign at the head of the driveway was also painted one day; it had every swear word in the book, along with threats, etc., and in the end said, "Jesus Lives." Some of our neighbors were disgusted and enraged by the act, and they wanted to hunt down those who did it and prosecute them. I told them, "What for? They are already in hell, with that kind of thought process. I feel sorry for them." To think Jesus would inspire profanity, destruction of personal property and the judgment and condemnation behind that act, is about as unconscious as one can get.

One of the things we were also dealing with were chemtrails—biologicals sprayed overhead by jets during major UFO conventions, and now on entire cities. I had picked up an intestinal virus the likes of which no doctor had ever seen; my intestines became swollen to the extent that they burst out, creating a hernia.

I now knew about the biologicals, and how the dark forces can activate them with psychotronics and HAARP technology like they did with my friend Choi. I felt the energies several times coming at me. It was as if I were being nuked or microwaved, and somehow they had targeted my room. I often had to move the location where I slept at night, which seemed to help. These energies specifically zeroed in on certain areas in the house, which led me to believe they were mechanical in nature. I was also informed they could pinpoint certain frequencies, the enlightened ones, and send sickening or deadly energies from afar.

Many UFO investigators were coming down with cancer and heart attacks, at an alarming rate, just when they were going to spill the beans. My own body was failing, and despite all of my herbal and spiritual techniques, I could not go on much longer. I did a deep meditation and told God and the Masters that if I am to be of any further service, they needed to do their part. I agreed to do whatever was in alignment with the divine plan, even if it meant my demise. I was so weary and ill that I could not go on any further.

My financial assets were gone as well; the government had stripped everything away other than the Sanctuary. Having no other recourse, I totally surrendered to Spirit. Soon I began to feel a presence. It was very powerful, and although it did not manifest fully, I could see clairvoyantly the image of a yogi with bushy hair. He began to move his hand in a circular motion above the affected areas of my body, and I could feel energy swirling within my innards. The pain and swelling disappeared instantaneously. There were several other areas where I felt things actually leave my body. My prayers were finally answered.

My health returned, though I was not completely healed; I was told that in six days the rest of my body would heal, and that I had to continue to do my part. I asked the Yogi if I should come to India. He said, "No, your work is here." I fully understood.

I do not know the name of the bushy haired Yogi. Some say it was Sai Baba. There is much controversy about Sai Baba, as there is with anyone in the limelight. I have heard many stories calling him everything from God, to child molester, to charlatan. There are many cases where a very enlightened individual can posses siddhis or spiritual abilities, yet still be working out lessons in one aspect of life.

I can only recount my own personal spiritual experience, and I believe that each individual must make up their own mind, not from gossip or rumors, but from firsthand experience. I am a bit biased, of course, due to the healing I experienced, yet I have always stated that it is imperative for each individual to make their own personal God connection. Become that which you admire. There is nothing wrong with getting a little help along the way, however.

Maat, the Egyptian Goddess

I was in constant communication with Mary, Blaji, the Hathors and other divine feminine energies. What transpired later in my spiritual evolution was a blessing of divine feminine love that was overwhelming. It felt very familiar, as if I had experienced it before. I had always been fascinated with Egypt, and on several occasions I recalled past-life memories of having a bronze, muscular body, wearing a white Egyptian headdress, with a white sarong around my waist. The Sun was warm on my chest, and life was good. I felt very connected to the Sun and knew that spiritual energies emanated from it. Without the Sun, all life would cease. It was my connection to GOD.

I was on the road, staying at a friend's house. Serena was a very gifted astrologer and psychic. We often spoke about astrology, and I would ask her very challenging questions like, "Which takes precedence, the stars' influence or my free will?"

She would say, "Free will, yet the stars influence our decisions." I would ask about the different forms of astrology and how some forms did not align with the planets' positions according to their ephemeris. She would explain to me how Vedic astrology did align with the positions of the planets, and how other forms were created or changed in the past. I had not, for the life of me, been able to understand how, if the planets were not where they were said to be, they could influence us. Finally someone (Serena) answered my question.

As I passed a beautiful altar she had prepared, I saw a picture of Maat, the Egyptian goddess. It stopped me dead in my tracks; I could not take my eyes off it, and chills began to run down my spine. I knew I had to have a copy of that picture to meditate on, to find out what connection I had with her. Serena made a wonderful laser print and sent it to me. As soon as it arrived, I opened up the envelope and the same chills again began to flow down my spine. I put the picture in front of me and stared at it until my eyes began to lose focus.

The next thing I knew, the reunion with Maat, along with the full memories of a time when I attuned to her in the past, was awakened. Love began to wash over me in waves, rising exponentially in frequency until I felt that any more love would either kill me or cause me to ascend, never to return.

I brought my focus back to my body and the here and now. I could still feel the love pouring out to me, yet now it was being grounded and was easier to assimilate. I knew no harm would come to me, but being in the presence of a love so intense was overpowering; I knew I had to adjust to it.

This love was what I had searched for all my life on Earth, yet it was nowhere to be found. In truth, there is no comparison to the love of Spirit. Maybe one day it will exist on Earth; as above, so below. Maat is often depicted with a feather. There are two dishes suspended on a scale, upon which she weighs the feather against the soul to see if it can go to heaven. I think it is a message that we all need to lighten up.

A Greater Plan for the Planet

After becoming thoroughly disgusted with our present leadership on every level, I decided to do another all-day meditation. As usual, my friends on high appeared within and without. Within, I was shown the plans of the elite, who lust for power and wealth and who will not rest until they control, dominate and own everyone and everything.

I was also shown the awakening of some and the demise of others. I was shown how they couldn't sustain themselves during the end days of the vibrational lifting, and how they would resort to invasive and deadly technology to maintain their control. All of their attitudes, emotions and deeds will be greatly amplified. It would be as if all of their karma descended upon them very rapidly. Their health would fail and they would age rapidly.

All of their technology used to stop the awakening and healing process would eventually be rendered useless by a greater spiritual technology beyond their wildest imagination. Even the high-tech methods of healing that they have hoarded and kept from the masses will not work, because they forget one thing: Consciousness is the underlying factor in disease. Their bodies would fail, for every disease has its mental and emotional counterpart. I was also shown how many would go mad when their plans went awry.

I was shown the Master Yeshua ben Joseph (Jesus) with legions of Masters wearing multicolored robes, starting their forward march. I was shown the spiritually and technologically-advanced ETs playing their part as well, set up in their ships over the Earth's grid, ready to power up the entire planet. They had full use of creational energies; powers and abilities far beyond any black projects the dark hearts were creating on Earth. I was told that in time there would be an inversion or implosion, so to speak; all would reap what they had sown. There would be a tremendous wave of light, and the material-minded that identified only with the body and personality would not fare well. That level of mind would cease. I was told that just as tyranny was targeting others, it too shall be targeted energetically in the last days.

Only those who had made their own personal God connection, empowered others and served unselfishly in the awakening and healing process would understand and maintain consciousness during the process. I was also told to be patient and keep the faith, for this day is soon coming.

Tyranny will be no more. The preservation of higher consciousness and the environment will be the new order of the day. The thousand-year peace will come upon the land. This is a time of preparation for the fifth world, the Age of GOD, and we all have to prepare spiritually, mentally, emotionally and physically for exciting times in the days to come. To this I dedicate the rest of my life.

From an Alien Perspective

There are many that ask the question, "If there are aliens, why don't they land on the White House lawn, or during the Super Bowl?" To help us understand the answer, let us look at it from an advanced alien perspective. Let's conduct a mythical interview with Halial, Supreme Ambassador and Captain of the Galactic Consortium.

"I am Halial. When we came to study Earth, we found many interesting rituals we are still trying to understand. When we first came, we saw a large gathering of people sitting in a multilevel circular structure. This formation is good to unify energies and unite people in a common good. The people of Earth were all watching other Earth humans on a field of grass. These Earth humans divided themselves into two teams. They ran as fast as they could and tried to inflict as much damage as possible, slamming into each other over control of a dead animal skin filled with air. The humans in the multilevel structure also seemed to be divided, cheering for one side or the other while eating what analysis has shown us to be stuffed intestines of another animal, filled with the meat from the animal that used to wear the skin they were fighting over. They also drank a depressant, a liquid that made them act really strange and pee a lot.

"At other times, they sit in the same circular building and watch other Earth humans hit another stuffed animal hide with a wooden stick and then run around in circles. This might be an ancient Sufi ritual.

"They also fight over possession of another larger inflated animal skin and toss it through a hoop. In other places, they take turns kicking the dead animal skin around. I wonder if they know it is already dead. We don't understand why they would unify in a circle, then divide or idolize and fight over a dead animal skin. They seem to be obsessed with competition, domination and control.

"We decided to find the leadership of these primitive

people. We went to a large round white building that our scans showed to be the center of government. We scanned to find intelligence and integrity. What we found instead was corruption, dishonesty, obsession with drugs and sex, and long histories of engaging in actions that were very harmful to humanity and the Earth, even to the point of selling arms to both sides of wars they inspired.

"It seems that Earth humans worship and exalt this kind of behavior, because their leadership is a reflection of it. In our search to find a higher authority we found there was the elite: several families that run everything behind the scenes. Our scans showed them to be even more corrupt; their lust for power and material wealth was insatiable and they would not rest until they owned and controlled everyone and everything.

"We decided to find the protectors, those who were sworn to protect the citizens. We first tried the military, then the civilian agencies. What we found out was that they were also controlled by the elite, and cooperated with the plans of the elite. Even if it meant mass genocide or harming their own families and friends, these agencies would employ deadly force on whomever the elite asked them to. It had something to do with an oath to God and country. We have not yet figured out what killing the other expressions of God has to do with God's will, or how it serves the country to diminish freedom or create pain, suffering and loss to those within the country. We think it has something to do with the worshipping of dominance and control, incorrectly associating it with intelligence and power.

"What we found is that there was something else people worshipped even more than those who controlled the dead animal skin: there were these little green pieces of paper. The focus on these little green pieces of paper took up most of their thought processes. Even their actions and energies were mostly spent in acquiring these paper pieces. What little energy was left was used primarily for unsuccessful attempts at mating. What we also could not understand is how so many believed their survival depended on these green pieces of paper.

"The elite controlled and printed these little green pieces of paper. We found it amazing that people would trade objects of tangible value for them. They would even destroy their environment and each other for these papers. All attempts to assist people in cleaning up the air, water and land through free energy and other methods have been met with violent opposition. We even picked up a few humans throughout history and taught them the basic universal principles necessary for a healthy society and environment. We then left them as way-showers, but the other people killed them and later created a religion around them, altering their message to fit their needs.

"We shared with them our way, which would have created a quantum leap in evolution. Our leaders are chosen according to their spiritual awareness and dedication to service. We honor our children's unique purpose, and give them everything they need to excel in their gifts. They are also taught that there is no separation in life, to respect all life and to serve the Creator in all Creation. They willingly share and give back to society.

"We have transcended all material lack, and live in abundance. All attempts to share this knowledge on Earth have been met with violent resistance. We would show up in our triangular ships, only to find Earth humans unreachable. They were too caught up in another triangle: the victim-savior-persecutor triangle. They would not even question the role projected upon them, but act it out in an endless loop.

"Attempts by other benevolent off-world visitors were also met with dishonesty, violence and ill intent. It seems that all the Earth human wants is advanced weaponry to evolve further into the worship of control and dominance. We decided Earth humans were not to be engaged, but were to be isolated until further study was made. We quarantined the solar system and set up beacons to warn others not to land or engage this primitive society."

Orbs, Light Spheres and Probes

One of the phenomena happening at the Sanctuary was the appearance of orbs, or light spheres. These light spheres were photographed by guests on a regular basis. Some could see them and some could not, yet they would often appear on film for all to see. It is not uncommon to see them darting about the grounds in purple or electric blue colors. Many of the guests, while in meditation and while reading inspirational books, see them and feel inspired by their presence.

I was in deep meditation and my nephew, who was eight years old at the time, saw a golden orb hovering over my head. I asked him to go into the orb and tell me what he saw. He said he saw Jesus. I asked him what Jesus was saying. He said, "God is love, that is all, God is love, over and over." At the time I was having a telepathic contact with Jesus.

Light spheres are often associated with angels and ETs. In even the orthodox definitions of angels they are said to have superhuman abilities. They have healing and telepathic abilities, the ability to manifest, and the ability to bi-locate and be in several places at once. They eat, drink, sleep and even fight. They are known to appear in glowing spheres of light. I have found many people are experiencing these orbs and light spheres as the veils get thinner and the other planes and dimensions begin to merge.

There are many skeptics concerning these phenomena, yet while some of their arguments in certain circumstances hold true, most do not. These spheres are brilliant; they are seen moving behind trees, with branches casting shadows on the orbs. This proves that they have substance and are a distance away from the camera, not a dust particle or water spot on the lens.

They come in every size, shape and color, and display intelligence. Some pictures of them are taken indoors, which also removes the rain, snow or dust particle theories. One

Orbs at the Sanctuary

frame they are there, another they are not; therefore again it cannot be water spots on the lens.

The orbs are very attracted to soft energies. Females and children seem to attract them the best. They can be called in at will, where before and after shots show clearly that there was nothing present before calling upon them. Common sense and a reasonable mind dictate there is definitely something to these phenomena.

There have been many observations of paranormal activity at the ranch: large, golden energy beings often followed by smaller blue beings. There have been strange green lights photographed by guests with what looked like light ladders going up into the sky.

One of the most interesting events was when we were tending to a burn pile. I was hosing it down with a friend,

Plasma field orbs

and I was feeling a presence. Something was observing us, and I tuned into it and looked right at it. It was crouched behind a small bush about 40 feet away. It realized we were on to it and it stood up. It was a blend of brown and orange, under four feet tall, and it started to glow. The body began to become transparent, showing what looked like veins surrounding a light body. It then vanished. I turned to my friend and asked her, "Did you see that?"

She said, "What was it?" I asked her what she saw, to confirm my own observations. She said, "I saw a small being stand up, it was orange, it seemed to have veins right before it started to glow, and vanished."

Due to the high vibration of the land and the vortex there are ongoing paranormal activities at the ranch. I do not know who or what every thing is, yet I do know that it is a big universe we live in, and there are other planes and dimensions with civilizations much different than ours. Some exist right alongside of us in the unseen. The veils are so thin between worlds at the Sanctuary that these other worlds and beings can be experienced, and in some cases photographed.

Sky Watches, Kids and Marshmallows

We decided to open the ranch to whoever wanted to see UFOs firsthand. We would hold guided meditations and drumming circles around night campfires in order to unify and lift the energies—all necessary steps to engaging benevolent, spiritually advanced beings. The ships would come in high up, scan the group consciousness, and then come down a little lower. If fear was present or the group consciousness was not unified, they would often stay high in the heavens.

Many UFO investigators would come as skeptics and demand proof. I would show them the pictures and videos of the ships, then tell them if they want proof, to go out and meditate. "Ask them yourself," I'd say. "It is not up to me whether or not they decide to show themselves. It is up to you, and your willingness to rise up to their level. They will assist you as long as you are trying; it is your choice, and they will not trespass on free will."

In each case, the skeptics would be a little put off at first, but curiosity would eventually get the better of them. Sooner or later they would be out meditating under the clear night sky, asking for the ETs to grant them an audience. In each case it was given, and many returned home with their own photos, videos and firsthand experience.

We would also take them through a process of clearing away personal blocks and patterns, paving the way for their own telepathic contact. Now instead of investigators, they were contactees. This hampered their future impartial investigations, because now they were tapped-in. Score one for enlightenment.

It became a cat-and-mouse game for the military. They would send in the jets and helicopters and we would say to our guests, "Just be patient. When they leave, the ETs will return." The ETs would never engage the military; they just took the high road and left. We were told over and over that the ETs would love to land and assist humanity, but until humanity chooses peace as a collective and changes its policy towards off-world visitors, they will continue to come and go as elusive phantoms to the people who are unconscious or of ill intent.

I asked one day if the military was a threat to them, with its back-engineered technology. Blaji said no and demonstrated complete air superiority over a military jet that vectored in on her ship. As it approached, she merely vanished, and reappeared on his tail as he passed. She then flew up his tailpipe, dissipating into a cloud of white vapor all around his jet. I would have given anything to see the pilot's reaction.

One of the most fascinating phenomena I have seen demonstrated over and over is the innocence of a child, and its effect on the ETs. We would often have my nieces and nephews or other children of friends come to the meditations and drumming circles.

One night a child of a friend of mine lifted up his toasted marshmallow and said, "Here, mister spaceman. I have a toasted marshmallow just for you." The innocence and heartfelt gift from a child brought three ships down in full view of the entire group. Marshmallows and children became an integral part of sky watches from then on.

I believe it is important that each of us become like a child again. Regain that innocence, that sense of awe and openness. Maybe the Biblical passage saying we must become like one of these, the children, to enter the kingdom of heaven, also applies to the kingdom of space.

The ETs and those who exist right alongside us in other planes and dimensions are patiently waiting to walk among us. But only when it is safe and we choose to end our competitive, warring ways on each other and the environment, will this become a reality. To some special individuals, it already is a reality. We call many of them children.

The Chase

I awoke to a beautiful sunrise, with billowing clouds rising up from Mt. Adams with yellow, orange, violet and purple hues. I stretched my arms back, and was invigorated by the clean mountain air. It was a beautiful day, and I was determined nothing was going to screw it up.

After breakfast I decided to go into town. A beautiful talk show host named Shine decided to drive me into town after an interview. On our way down from the mountain, winding our way through the forest on Hwy 141, I noticed a white BMW behind us. I immediately felt we were being followed. I told Shine to pull over and let him pass. She did and he went by very slowly, then shot off down the road. As we went around another turn he was there waiting again, pulling out behind us. This confirmed my suspicions.

I asked Shine again to pull over along the river, and the white BMW again passed us, only this time I told her to pull out and follow him. We were coming to a fork in the road, which leads to either White Salmon or Hood River. I decided to go to Hood River, yet I told Shine "Don't put on your blinker. Do not even slow down...wait until he is committed to White Salmon beyond the fork ,and then make a sharp right." Shine did exactly as I wished, and we watched the BMW slam on the brakes and make a U turn.

We again pulled over along the side of the road behind some trees, only to watch the BMW speed by. I told Shine to pull out, and now again we were behind him. I could see a very distressed driver looking in his rearview mirror over and over to see if it was us. He turned left at Hwy 14, knowing that was the closest way to either town. We followed him, and again I instructed Shine to not signal or slow down until we hit the bridge to Hood River. If he were to take the bridge, he would be stuck with no way to turn around. If not, we would take the bridge.

The BMW driver passed the bridge very slowly, waiting to see if we would follow. We took a sharp right onto the bridge, and the BMW, after passing the bridge, slammed on the brakes, doing another U turn on 14, then proceeded on to the bridge a few cars back.

As we passed the toll booth, I told the operator I wanted to pay for the white BMW a few cars back, because he is having a bad day. The operator did as instructed, and we looked back to see the driver shaking his head and turning onto Hwy 84 heading towards Portland. I turned to Shine and said. "That was fun, wonder what the rest of the day has to offer."

Shine laughed and shook her head in amusement. She asked me, "Do all your days start out this way?"

I told her, "No, this one started out great, and I did not want anyone to steal it from me."

We often had fun with the Feds. I would talk on the phone, knowing they were listening, and speak about how everyone, no matter what agency they work for, is going to have to make a choice. The choice would be whether they served humanity, God and country or some elite group of people who care nothing about humanity, God or country. Each within their soul would have to make a choice. We often lectured them, acting as if we did not know they were listening.

The funniest thing we would do is to say the ships are landing tonight at 11:00. They are going to give us the technology. At 10:30 there would be bizarre trucks and cars parked along the east side of the ranch. We would see others to the north as well. I would often circle around them and come up from behind and ask them if they were watching those crazy people who lived there. I would say, "Keep an eye on them; who knows what they are up to."

Once there was a man in a Ford Pinto, with Gucci shoes and a communication headset on. He was far too well dressed for our area. He was parked along the river on the east side. I could overhear him talking about us, saying it does not look like there is any activity. When we walked by him I could not contain myself, and burst out laughing. He looked at us, and I turned around and said, "Come on! A Ford Pinto? No one drives a Ford Pinto. It is so unobvious that it's obvious."

The Art Bell Show

There had been many radio and TV interviews. Jeff Rense Sightings on the radio was one of the first. Several others followed along, with ABC, FOX, The History Channel and Evening Magazine all doing very favorable coverage of the ongoing UFO sightings and contacts at the Sanctuary. It was aired in Mexico and Germany as well. We were even featured in both UFO Magazines on more than one occasion, in both the US and the UK. The Art Bell Show, with over 20 million listeners, I would have to say was the peak experience. The first interviews with Ian Punnet went well, yet when it comes to talk shows concerning UFOs and the paranormal, Art is the king. It was a golden opportunity to get the message out.

The morning before the show, the Sanctuary was visited by two marine warthogs...low flying bombers. They buzzed the main lodge, as before, tipping their wings, showing us they were fully armed and ready to do business. I could just hear the show beginning with, "James will not be appearing tonight due to two US jets bombing the Sanctuary." This would be a tough one to explain. It is also tough to explain the law against having contact with aliens when the government stance is that they do not exist. How can they arrest you for having a contact with what according to them is a fictitious entity?

It is just like the laws against free energy generators and motors. They say it is impossible, yet if you build one they confiscate it and put you in jail, or you and your family disappear. Meanwhile the environment is collapsing, the air, water and land is polluted, and you are going to war over foreign oil. These points were all raised on the Art Bell Show.

I was given an opportunity to talk about our ancient ancestors and the UFO connection. The petroglyphs, hieroglyphs, frescos painted on church walls, even the bible and other sacred books all prove there was a strong historical off-world influence on today's civilization. We covered the 2,000+ eye witnesses that have come to the ranch, some of which are top physicists, having a few investigators and witnesses come on the show. We also covered the many contacts and information given by the ETs concerning their origins and intentions.

Basically the benevolent, spiritually and technologically advanced ETs, which I refer to as our ancient ancestors, the Star Nations or the greater family of man, only want one thing: They want us to stop warring on each other and the environment. It is their desire that we continue to evolve spiritually and clean up our environment. Everyone was waiting for the big message from the stars, yet the message was delivered over and over by every master from every culture that ever walked the Earth.

The message was delivered to over 20 million listeners this time, and the rest is up to them. The show began with a delay, due to a man claming he was part of a recovery operation of a downed ET craft in Alaska. He was a decoy to delay the interview. During the show our server and website underwent an incredible assault. The server is run by a man very adept at security, due to handling military sites in the past. It stood up to the assaults until the phone company mysteriously decided to shut down the main lines, which caused a bottleneck and the site to be inaccessible. Nonetheless, the orders for books and videos came flooding in. The message went out.

We were told it was by far, if not the best, one of the best interviews ever on the Art Bell Show. Art himself said the very same thing. People everywhere were commenting on how excited Art was when he saw the videos. The ships were lighting up, stopping, making right angle turns and responding to the people on the ground. The interactive qualities were undeniable. The UFOs came in every color and size, and did phenomenal aerial displays. There were giant triangles as well, showing undeniable proof these are off-world visitors and beyond any back-engineered models held in secret government facilities.

We had hoped that after delivering the message the support would follow. In their heart of hearts, that people would understand the importance of the events happening at the Sanctuary, as well as the necessity to get behind the awakening and healing of humanity and the Earth. The events unfolding at the Sanctuary were unprecedented in human history. They had the potential to change the destiny of humanity and the Earth, moving both in a positive direction, the upward spiral. We were given the opportunity for a quantum leap in evolution and the invitation to join the rest of the universe in peace.

It seems the beer, TV and football games, along with the trappings of social consciousness, have numbed the sheeple into complicity. Rather than being bothered with universal peace, an end to disease, war and poverty, all they wanted to do is go on with business as usual. Despite the collapsing environment, it was as if ministering to a herd of cattle. A couple looked up for a moment, then went back to grazing. Well, we all know where the cattle and sheep end up.

Freedom has a price, and enlightenment does not come through a TV. If you want peace and freedom, you are going to have to make a steadfast stand for it. If you want enlightenment, unplug your TV and read. Seek out the enlightened ones, the radical few with their own minds; step out of the herd. Maybe a little Art Bell is in order.

The Landings

Something everyone has been waiting for finally occurred. There were two fully documented landings, with multiple eyewitnesses. The ships were enormous. They defied all the laws of physics, morphing in and out of existence, splitting into two, three and as many as four ships of equal size and light intensity. They moved over the top of Mt. Adams on the southeastern flank, then descended over sheer cliffs and down glaciers to the bottom of the mountain, while putting on a display of light and movement beyond belief. They responded to the witnesses on the ground.

When one witness said, "We will be up, right there on the mountain this summer," the ship responded with an expansion of light ten times its usual intensity. This happened on several occasions. The ship was clearly responding to the guests. Twice guests said, "We love you," and the ship flashed back in recognition.

The witnesses asked, "Why won't they come here and land?" I told them there is a law against full-blown contact. If they were to land here, I could be thrown in jail, my property would be confiscated, and I would have to pay a $5,000 fine. It would go to the head of NASA, who would determine whether I had had a contact or not. If they deemed it valid, you would not see me for a while, and the spiritual retreat would be taken over by unconscious individuals putting an end to things.

Those whom we have chosen to greet them have not met the protocols necessary for contact. It takes an open mind, loving heart and pure intentions. Greeting them with aggression, ill intent or with an agenda other than service to humanity and the Earth has and will continue to be unsuccessful with the benevolent, spiritually and technologically advanced beings. Until the masses come to understand this and hold their leaders to these ideals, there will not be a reunion with the benevolent ones. There will only be lower-level contacts that are not in the highest and best good of the people and the planet.

If Earth humanity wants to reunite with the rest of the universal family of man, there has to be a change in consciousness and action. Spiritual ambassadors will have to be designated. Guidelines will have to be established concerning the exchange of knowledge and technology, directing them only in service to humanity and the Earth. There will have to be impeccable integrity in these matters. The benevolent ETs have allowed us to document their presence.

The next step is to create a military stand-down and cease all aggression towards them and their ships. Then ambassadors and galactic exchange centers need to be established. When this is done they will land and walk hand-in-hand with us, assisting humanity with a quantum leap in evolution.

It is a two-way street. Earth humanity must do its part. They will not trespass on free will. This is an unprecedented event, a golden opportunity, and any reasonable mind would jump at the chance. It could mean the end of disease and poverty, and the beginning of free energy and the complete restoration of the planet. The doors to vast, incredible, unknown worlds within this universe, as well as other planes and dimensions, will open. It is time to choose.

Soul Mates

There has been much talk about soul mates. It seems everyone is in the elusive search for the one that is going to make them happy, rather than becoming the mate they wish to attract. When I used to hear other people say that so and so is my soul mate, I wanted to gag. Not really gag, but in my head I would think, "Boy are they going to be disappointed when the fantasy stops and reality sets in. When La La Land fades and the honeymoon phase is over, we will see." I have seen too many times people misplace all their love, joy and happiness outside of themselves in their mates, only to find pain and misery when their mate did not add up to their expectations and could not meet the unreasonable demands placed upon them.

When you truly meet your soul mate, there are no assurances of happily ever after. In fact, in most cases it is quite the contrary. The energies between soul mates create a quickening. Anything in the seven seals or chakras which is not vibrating or does not match the higher frequencies is amplified or quickened. If one mate is more spiritually advanced than the other, it creates confusion. This can result in emotional outbursts, or a complete shutting down. The fear, old wounds and traumas from past experience are triggered, and the spiritual growth is often too fast for the one lagging behind to handle. Such was the case when I met my soul mate.

Her name was Meagan. I was in deep meditation at the ranch, and I saw her face. She was beautiful and looked like an angelic being, yet in the physical. Two days later I had a dream, and in the dream I was sitting across from her at a coffee shop. Another day passed, and I felt very strong guidance to go to Hood River, Oregon, the town to which we go to shop, eat and entertain ourselves. I drove by the coffee shop and did not see anyone, so I went about my business. The whole day I had a high feeling of expectation, the feeling you get before something big happens in your life. There was a part of me that knew she was in town somewhere, and the image of her at the coffee shop kept appearing in my mind's eye.

I decided to go and get a mocha and sit on the bench for a while to see what transpired. As I sat on the bench I looked just behind me and to the right, and there she was, sitting in a chair with her long legs and angelic body, just like the vision. Her face matched the vision, and I stared at her in shock. I did not know what to say. It all seemed surreal and somehow the words just came to me. I said, "Hello, how are you this morning?" I was fighting back my soul, which wanted to jump out of my body, hug and dance with her.

She was very cautious, and it was very clear that although interested, she did not have the same feelings. We talked for a while, and finally she began to feel very comfortable with me. She expressed an interest in the ranch and the ongoing events there, which opened the door to an invitation to come and share in the experience.

From that point on it was an emotional roller coaster between heaven and hell. My desire to be with her was so intense it would overtake me at times, and it was all I could do to hold it at bay. Although she was with me physically, she could never join me emotionally or spiritually. Although we slept together for almost two years, we never had sex, there was this wall between us I could never penetrate. I would awaken at night and see her perfect body, the moonlight on her face, the innocence of sleep, and want to awaken her to tell her how much I loved her, but I knew she would reject me as she had in the past.

I could feel our connection on the highest levels, yet could never bring it down to Earth. This was the hell. To know what was possible, have it right there beside you, yet that wall would never let it manifest. It was like holding back the pressures of a massive dam; very few can let go and flow with the river. They end up clinging to the past, what is safe and known, a golden opportunity missed.

I wish I could say it had a happy ending, but the energies of the ranch, the vortex and the quickening were too much for her. Who knows what the future may bring? I will always hold the vision and remember the possibility and the overwhelming love I experienced in her presence. My grandmother always said you have to kiss a few toads before you find your prince. I had hoped the toad kissing was over, but she is still in the pond somewhere gaining wisdom through experience.

The Trip up the Mountain

Before Meagan left, we had a visitor come to the ranch. On the surface he was a really nice guy, but surrounding him were some very negative beings. They would show themselves at times as an overlay, which other guests would see and then come to me completely freaked out. If anyone saw The Fifth Element and the grotesque warriors, they looked very much the same. They seemed to be able to possess people and utilize them to disrupt. We did several spiritual clearings but for some reason this group would not let go of this man.

I had to go to Eugene, Oregon, and work on a crystallized oxygen water project. I told Meagan she could stay at the ranch as long as she liked, considering it her home, and then I left, bound for Eugene. Meagan called and told me the troubled man wanted to take her on a hike up on the mountain. I told her that by no means should she go with him. There are forces at play you know not of, and you are not strong enough to deal with them yet. Please keep your distance from him until I get home. She took my warning as jealousy or an attempt to control her, and up the mountain she went.

I had a really bad feeling all day, and could not shake it. I called the ranch and a friend answered and told me Meagan went up the mountain with the troubled one. I now knew what the foreboding feeling was. I knew it was an attempt by the darker forces to take her over. They are very threatened when soul mates come together, especially those on a spiritual path. Together they have the spiritual energies to alter planetary consciousness.

When Meagan and I were together, people would take photographs. The white light would spiral off our crown chakras into a giant vortex above our heads. You could see angelic guides and Masters from the next realm or dimension above us. Light spheres would appear all around us. I understand now why our coming together was such a threat.

I began to pray, knowing she was in trouble. I asked all the Arch Angels, Cazekiel, Jesus, Mary, everyone to please do whatever was necessary to protect her. I saw myself leaving my body at light speed and merging with her. The man was asking her to heal him, begging her to put her hand on his heart. The negative beings were all around him, hoping he would make a bridge to her soul.

Just before he put his hand on her chest, a brilliant light blasted from her heart and knocked him to the ground. The energies were so intense it completely incapacitated him, with no control of his body. His bowels and bladder let go as well, and there he lay in his own fecal matter. It was not a pretty sight. Meagan had to clean him up and drive him home, because he still had no control of his body and was very weak.

I did not have to say a thing when I returned. She still seemed to be in a bit of shock. My world was a little too intense for her, and she was thrust into an event she was not ready or prepared for. I was hoping to teach and train her in these matters. Yet I was already pushing her a little too fast for her own comfort.

Max the Wizard

If someone were to tell me the story of how I met Max I would smile and say, "Okay," and look around for the men in white coats.

I was very adept at out of body travel. Your spirit on that level seems to know who you need to meet, and where they are. I was meditating and kept getting the message that "there is a wise one here on Earth who can help you." I was suffering from an intestinal infection, a virus or bacteria that seemed to act like no other pathogen. If you treated it like a bacteria, it mutated into a virus. If you treated it like a virus, it became bacteria. It seemed to dine on antibiotics, and was taking its toll, making me very ill. I could spiritually override it and continue to be mobile, but my body just could not kick it.

In the meditation I found myself leaving my body and ending up hovering over two people in a jet liner on the way to Texas. Max was joined by a friend, whose name was Harold. Max was the first to recognize me hovering there, and poked Harold, who was half asleep. Harold, half awake, looked up and said, "I know that guy." He had been to the ranch before for a sky watch, and recognized my face. Max said "I want to meet him; he is looking for me."

I received a phone call from Harold telling me there was a German physicist who wanted to meet me. I had a strong feeling I needed to meet this man, yet was still unaware he was the one in the plane. Spirit works in strange ways when it comes to bringing people together with common soul purposes.

I went to Eugene to meet Max and was waiting at the Steel Head Brew Pub. At the time Max would never meet people at his lab; it was too dangerous, and there were problems in the past with thieves and unscrupulous men who wanted to steal his technologies. Not only did Max have phenomenal, what can only be called miracle healing technologies, he also had energy devices which certain elements in our government and other industries did not want to get out. His lab was blown up electrically by taking all the electrical power from the block and sending it through his lab. His car was stolen and rifled through and his family was threatened. I could not blame him for taking precautions.

What is sad is that we have the fuel-less engines, anti and counter gravity, as well as the cures for most diseases. We have the technologies to clean up and restore the environment to its pristine beauty. Unfortunately, these technologies cut into the profits of the Oil and Pharmaceutical companies, just as peace cuts into the War Industry profits.

Max was crossing the street, and we both recognized each other immediately. We had lunch and Max felt comfortable with me, and we went back to the lab. Max mixed up a formula and gave it to me, along with the crystallized oxygen water. I felt immediate relief. Something I had been battling with for years, suddenly like magic was gone. I felt my life forces coming back almost immediately.

Max explained to me about the formula. He said he took one look at me and knew what the problem was. It was a biological agent generated to make people like me go away. His oxygen water kills bacteria and virus at the same time. There is nowhere to hide. He showed me a polluted water sample full of pathogens. He added the water and through the microscope I could see the pathogens explode and transform to a crystalline structure. I asked him what the crystalline structure was and he said, "It becomes food for the body, rather than a toxic die off." I was shocked, and asked if this would work on all pathogens, and he said yes.

I then asked, "Do you know what you have here?" and he said, "I do, but the trick is how we get it out to the public." I spent the next six years doing just that. I was shown many other devices, which were fuel-less and put out enormous amounts of energy. I also saw a motor for a flying vehicle. One of his motors revved up too high when he was distracted by a telephone call. As it began its ascent, Max tried to grab it. It broke his arm and shot into the sky. I asked him where it landed and he said that it didn't. The last time he saw it, the motor was headed for the Sun. This was, of course, after leaving a very large hole in his roof and a broken arm.

I saw Max demonstrate the motor to other physicists and some former rocket scientists. He would tell them that if they could figure it out, they could have it. They spent weeks taking it apart, looking at it under a microscope. There was no science to explain these devices. Max would always say, "You don't get science from a book; true science comes to you."

What is sad about these amazing technologies is the field of free energy itself. Many in the field, just like ufology, are not what they seem to be. There are those who offer large sums of money to anyone who will demonstrate an "over unity" device. Max demonstrated his motor, which was far beyond over unity. In fact, his problem was never generating the energy...it was how to keep a governor on it.

Nonetheless, those offering the prize money never seemed to have it, or tried to steal the devices later. Every time we met with someone who claimed to be a humanitarian, the next thing we knew we were meeting with the military. Max would make it very clear that he was not building war toys. He turned down millions, due to the character of the people he was dealing with. In this I have to admire his integrity. Most people would not turn down such an offer, and the technology would never benefit the public or see the light of day.

There were other so-called humanitarians who in truth worked for the oil companies or wanted to be the go-between with a large finder's fee. Each time we would find their clients had no intention of using the technology for humanitarian purposes. It was earmarked for military application or to be shelved and kept from the public.

After more death threats and the constant harassment by people of no integrity, Max finally gave up and dismantled all of his engines, scattering them about the country. Many say, "Give it to me, I have connections, I will take the heat and get out the technology," yet each time when the heat was on they were the first to disappear.

Back on the Mountain Again

After spending six years working long, hard hours trying to get out the healing technologies, sometimes weeks at a time without rest, I decided I had to take my leave and return to the mountain. To awaken and to try to bring that awakening back to the masses takes its toll. The material mind and what I call the dark network is rooted deep. Minds driven by greed, profit and power were many, true humanitarians were few. I used to tell a joke: If vegetarians eat veggies what do humanitarians eat? So far all I have seen them eat are humans. There is a lot of talk, but as that little old lady in the commercials would say, "WHERE'S THE BEEF?"

I saw a lot of selfishness but very little selflessness. I felt like Lot when the Angels told him to find ten good men. After not finding one, he left for the mountain. I wasn't very good at finding a good woman either. I remembered again what a wise mature woman told me. She said, "As soon as you meet your next girl friend, take her out to the pond and drown her. Only then will she understand you and be on the same page."

What brings me great solace is the friends and family unseen, and a few real friends and family on Earth. I have also had a peek into the future and know it is humanity's destiny to heal and awaken, just as it is Earth's destiny. We will join the Greater Family of Man throughout the universe. It is only a matter of time. Those who want to awaken, heal and rise to the occasion can climb the mountain.

Never Give up

Back on the mountain I licked my wounds, pulled the knives out of my back, and settled into the forgiveness and compassion mode. I always remembered what Isis said: "No matter how much it hurts you have to keep loving, for love is the only way through."

I focused my thoughts on the Source, Cazekiel, Jesus, Mary, Blaji, Melia and the Beautiful Many Masters, merging with them and letting the old wounds and traumas fall away. In each case, as the wisdom was gained from the experience it would settle in the soul, and the pain and confusion would leave. I would be stronger for the experience.

I felt my energies building; the effects to the body were also healing, and once again I vowed never to put myself in these situations. The stress that comes with them is a killer, literally. I continued working on the mastery of loving detachment and non-judgment. The feminine energies would always come to me and fill any void beyond anything I had ever experienced on Earth. I realized it was wrong of me to expect a heavenly love on Earth, although I do not discount the possibility of it.

Most have never remembered their true nature, their God nature. The makeup of their chosen identity still is filled with fear, wounds, traumas and wrong conclusions from past experiences. They are embroiled in social consciousness, still seeking approval and acceptance from society, which is futile. Society will always judge you according to its values and beliefs, which are far from noble and enlightened. The only real acceptance and approval must always come from within, from a source that never judges you, and loves you unconditionally.

Enlightenment has never come through a book or another person. It is a personal journey, it is a living God we seek, and to truly find oneself and ones own unique purpose, one has to go within.

Nature is the best church one will ever find. The trees don't judge you or project their beliefs and desires on you. The rock has just observed for eons. The stream does not hesitate on its journey, and flows around all obstacles to merge with the sea. The raindrop and the ocean become one, just as we will all eventually become one with the one consciousness that encompasses all consciousness. The mountain always reminds me of this, and once centered in this consciousness the doors open to other planes and dimensions, worlds beyond your wildest dreams.

Plemaria

While in meditation I was contacted by another Pleiadian woman. She was not as advanced as Blaji, who is over two million years ahead of us in the time flow as we know it, and on the sixth dimension. This woman felt very familiar.

I never met a Pleiadian I didn't like, for they are all exquisitely loving and wise, yet this one was different. She was on the etheric level, much closer to my physical reality. She told me her name was Plemaria, and she had been looking for me for eons. Apparently she had bent the rules and gone against the prime directive, which does not allow physical contact unless granted in special cases, which have to be authorized by a higher council. She was observing me floundering on Earth, doubting myself and getting caught up in the dramas of social consciousness.

I found out later that when in LA on one of the many mercy missions with Max, she had appeared to me. I was in a restaurant, and a band was playing in the next room. Karen, Max's wife, loved to dance, and despite her humility she moved with the grace of an angel. The room was a bit crowded for my comfort, so I stood off to the side where there was a little open space and watched. After a few songs, a beautiful blonde walked up to me and laid one of the most passionate kisses on me I had ever experienced. I was spell bound, stunned, and as she turned to walk away, my hand slid across her waist and she was gone. I walked in the direction I had last seen her and she completely vanished. There is no way she could have made it to the door without me seeing her. Plemaria told me it was her; she could not bear watching me without doing something.

That kiss changed my entire life. It lifted me, reinstated my self-confidence, and made life worth living again. There was something to look forward to.

I learned from a great master who met his soul mate and found her to be a very wretched entity, that there was a way out. After being crushed by his earthly experience with his soul mate, which consisted of pain, deception and sadness, he decided to make GOD his soul mate. The feminine aspect of GOD filled the void, and he became complete and ascended. He said that when you accomplish this there are no limitations, everyone is your soul mate and the love flows through you like a river. Then you are free to love without attachment or expectations.

Plemaria was a love from long since past that had come to reunite with her lover. And who might that be, but I.

Addressing the Council

Blaji came to me and told me about the transgression of the rules. Plemaria had, let us say, fallen from the grace of the council due to paying an unauthorized visit to help me in a time of confusion. It was the talk of the community.

I asked Blaji who was in charge, and she gave me the name of the man who Plemaria answered to on the council. I asked Blaji if I could communicate with him, and she said of course; you know his name, use your telepathy.

I went into deep meditation and the thought came to me that I have friends in high places. I could use their influence and backing as long as I stay within universal law to help in this matter. I called on Cazekiel, referred to by an Andromedan as the God of Eternal Bliss. After all, the Pleiadians deeply respect the Andromedans, and often look to them for advice.

Once connected to Cazekiel I focused my attention on the high council. I sent them a message. "In the name of Cazekiel I wish to address the council." I waited and felt the attention of several great masters. Feeling their attention, I told them I wanted to speak concerning the matter of Plemaria breaking the prime directive and coming to my aid. I felt the request was granted. I then told them, "There is one law that supersedes all laws, and that is the law of love. Her act was done out of love; a love that was created on high, a union sanctified by the Source itself. This love supersedes the prime directive, and she is duty bound to follow the one law that supersedes all laws, which is the law of love. There was no argument, just silent contemplation.

"I remember my past. I was born from the very Source itself, as all were. I lived in the Andromedas, the Pleiades and Orion, just as I have lived many incarnations on Earth. The prime directive should not limit my access to my extended family.

"I wish there were more like her, because there are many

on Earth that are in great need of your help. They are good people, just a little confused and wounded. In some cases a little divine intervention would work miracles. I do not believe a prime directive as a blanket policy is correct; it needs to be on an individual basis. I see the necessity for the prime directive, and how it keeps the peace with other off-world beings that might take advantage of the people of Earth, yet this has already occurred. Lesser evolved beings had already greatly interfered with the evolution of Earth, and we could really use some help on high in this matter.

"It is not fair to the Earth herself, and she could really use some help in this matter as well. Her destiny is not to die, to experience environmental collapse and have her air, water and land poisoned by the lust for power and the greed of these degenerate souls. I also am aware of the action/reaction or karmic consequences these degenerate souls need to experience, and the lesson Nature will soon deliver, yet there are many that are right on the edge of awakening. They are worth a little extra effort, I being one of them.

"The extra effort of Plemaria should be honored, not admonished, because she operated according to the highest law, which is the law of love. Her actions were GOD-inspired and her soul had no other choice but to comply, even at the cost of losing respect from a council she loves and holds in the highest regard.

"In the name of Cazekiel I send blessings, love and joy, and honor the council's decision, knowing it will be of the highest love, a love that knows no boundaries. I also wish to extend on behalf of humanity of Earth, even those asleep, my deepest gratitude for all you have done assisting the Earth in its awakening and healing process. Blessing be to all of you."

The Council's Decision

Plemaria came to me again in my meditation. She said, "The Council has decided. I have been elevated to an ambassador position. It seems your speech did not fall upon deaf ears and closed hearts. It touched them deeply. This gives me more flexibility in our connection. They also honor you as an ambassador of the most high. In just a few months, we will be reunited. It brings me great joy to tell you this; my heart is singing.

The Earth will go through its healing and cleansing process. We cannot stop this process; it is her destiny. We can assist those who ask in these times.

It is prophecy that the Star Nations will return in the days of change. This prophecy will be fulfilled. The assistance Earth Humanity will receive will be phenomenal, yet it is still according to universal law. We cannot interfere in free will or the balancing of karma unless the lessons are learned and choices are made to forgive self for creating the karma and to forgive others for becoming the platform for one's lessons.

Those on the path of enlightenment and those who are in service to humanity and the Earth will receive the greatest assistance. It will be a joint effort, not a rescue. Many will be guided to move from certain areas. They must act on this guidance, without attachment to their homes, friends and family.

Denial is a luxury Earth Humanity can't afford in the days to come. We will do all we can to assist in this process, and the Earth will have its healing and fulfill its destiny, which is a thousand years of peace.

There will be a lot of unrest between now and then on every level. Now is the time to lovingly and joyously prepare, work together, and cooperate in the highest and best good of the people and the planet through this process."

Not the End; The Beginning of a New Era

A Final Note to the Reader

As I mentioned in the Foreword, this book was not written for self-aggrandizement, but to share my path and to help me put some major events into perspective. You may have found, as you read these pages, strong issues and emotions began to surface for you. Perhaps you experienced skepticism and disbelief, as I once did, before I developed reference points of my own.

Maybe you desire to drop everything and come follow me as your guru, or you feel outrage that I would dare to state certain ideas and truths. My only response here is that I am as human, as you are. You are your own guru, and only you know your own unique soul purpose, and must learn to lead yourself.

By putting out this book, I hope to offer some guidelines on how to transcend problems and limitations, and support those who are awakening and are having similar experiences. If you are now struggling with some issues, it is good that they have come up for scrutiny and healing.

You may not realize this yet, but you too are a powerful, loving, manifesting God/Goddess, and you lack nothing. You are the spark waiting to burst into the full flame of creation. I wish you the very best on your own awakening process, your own Journey back to Source.

Appendix

Bio of James Gilliland

James Gilliland is a minister, counselor, an internationally known lecturer, best selling author with the books, Reunion with Source, Becoming Gods, and The Ultimate Soul Journey. James appeared in Contact Has Begun, His Story, The History Channel, UFOs then and Now, UFO Hotspots, ABC, Fox News, BBC Danny Dyer Special, Paranormal State, ECETI Ranch a Documentary, and the new movie Thrive have all featured James and ECETI which he is the founder.

He has appeared on Coast to Coast, Jeff Rense, and to numerous other radio shows to mention also being the host of, As You Wish Talk Radio, www.bbsradio.com and Contact Has Begun, www.worldpuja.net. He is a facilitator of many Eastern disciplines, a visionary dedicated to the awakening and healing of Humanity and the Earth and teaches higher dimensional realities from experience.

For other books by James, DVD's, conferences, updates and more go to www.eceti.org